THE
SENSITIVITY
PHENOMENON

THE SENSITIVITY PHENOMENON

by
Joseph J. Reidy, M.D.

A PRIORITY EDITION

ABBEY PRESS
ST. MEINRAD, INDIANA 47577
1972

First published, 1972
© 1972 by Joseph J. Reidy, M.D.
Library of Congress Catalog Card Number: 72-89194
All rights reserved
Printed in the United States of America

Abbey Press
St. Meinrad, Indiana 47577

TABLE OF CONTENTS

INTRODUCTION

In recent years there has appeared a considerable number of group programs whose intent is to help people change and grow. Although these programs came from disparate sources and are called by many different names, they have intermingled and borrowed ideas and methods from one another, so that now they can be considered as one movement. I have chosen to call this movement *The Sensitivity Phenomenon.*

This book examines the important features of this phenomenon: its history, philosophy, methods, leaders and the results of its efforts. It is an attempt to evaluate the sensitivity training and encounter groups as they exist today.

For many reasons this evaluation is a difficult undertaking; it is often difficult to avoid straying from reality and objectivity. Sensitivity training and encounter groups have to do with the most important and the most personal concerns of mankind. They deal with the feelings of love and hate, the expressions of sex and aggression, the ways people live in families, social groups, work and religious groups. No aspect of living, feeling or relating is excluded from the agenda of these groups. To include so many things, to endeavor to solve so many problems, seems impossible. One way to accomplish so immense a task is to find some formula, some principle that will apply to all elements. The result usually will be an oversimplification, and an ignoring of those facts which do not fit the formula. This loss of objectivity has characterized the programs of many in the movement, so that, for example, the leaders of these programs feel their programs are suitable for everyone.

Lack of objectivity has also been a mark of some of the critics of the movement, those critics who judge that the excess of some leaders and programs apply to every leader and program in the movement. They judge the movement as a whole by some of the extremists and do not take the trouble to evaluate the leaders and programs which are more conservative in their methods, more modest in their claims, but have been helpful to many persons.

Another difficulty is that a person is likely to become threatened and defensive when dealing with these very personal matters. The advocates of these programs and their opponents have not always come to their positions on the basis of objective, verifiable data, but on the basis of feelings and convictions. When their feelings and convictions are challenged, they feel personally challenged; what is involved is not an impersonal scientific finding, but their pride and self-worth.

This is not all. The issues the movement concerns itself with are difficult to examine, matters on which it is difficult to get people to agree. Leaving aside political, social and religious points of view—which lie beyond my field—I am considering in this book only the psychological aspects of those things sensitivity training and encounter deal with and attempt to change. Within the fields of psychology and psychiatry there are controversies over many matters of theory and treatment, and astute scientists disagree on fundamental issues. In sensitivity training and the encounter movement there is often none of the caution and painstaking work of scientific inquiry. The advocates of some programs offer, without any attempt at verification, theories on complex psychological conditions, conditions which have not been adequately understood by experts. Without adequate research and controls they produce methods to help emotionally ill persons.

When writing about these matters which are so important and

about which we know so little, the danger is that one can become a polemicist. The literature on the movement, written by its practitioners and theorists as well as by its critics, has often been a polemical rather than a scientific one. I do not intend my presentation to be an original evaluation of sensitivity training and encounter, nor a research project. However, even though it is written for an audience wider than that of the scientific community, its purpose is scientific. I have attempted to present the available knowledge, to present what we know at this time, and to let this information decide the issues.

I have written many things critical of the offerings of these groups, but this does not mean that I am personally critical of the movement. Sensitivity training and encounter groups have developed from sound research and practice in group dynamics and group psychotherapy; I have pointed out how some programs and leaders misuse these concepts and methods. Under the banner of science the movement has often espoused ideas and practices of doubtful value, contradicting known scientific data, promoted by the techniques of salesmanship rather than those of scholarship. It is to the credit of many persons in this movement that they have again called attention to the multitude of unhappy persons, to the great emotional needs of so many people. Some groups have helped those who participated; others have been a disappointment to those who joined because of the unrealistic promises they made; others have been harmful to those who took part.

The groups which make up this movement have proliferated rapidly, have become a part of the business, educational and mental health fields, and have attracted much attention. Persons who are considering participating in these groups, those who are called upon to approve them as part of industrial, educational or treatment programs, need information to help them in deciding whether to participate in them or approve them. It is difficult for many persons to separate the defects and the dangers from the worthwhile contributions of the programs. The allegations of some of the advocates of sensitivity training and encounter and of some of its critics do not provide sufficient and reliable data.

An important principle—indeed, an essential one—of sensitivity training is that experiencing is the most reliable way of knowing. The proponents of sensitivity training would take a dim view of anyone making a statement about a program he has not participated in, a method he has not used. Carried to its logical end, this means that one could not make a decision about participating in a sensitivity training or encounter group on the basis of reading a report in the scientific literature, or a book such as this one. Without becoming involved in a discussion of epistemology, I would like to say only that it is true that participation, or experiencing, does bring a certain order of knowledge, but it is impossible for each person to verify through his own experience the multitude of things he needs to know in his life. Nor are all experiences wise or safe for all persons. The elements in sensitivity training and encounter are not all so unique, so far removed from the experiences of men, that they cannot be judged in other ways than by participating in the group programs. All of the elements of these programs have been part of psychological theories, of treatment methods, of group dynamics. They have been tried and have been evaluated.

My own direct experience with sensitivity training and encounter is limited to being in groups where some of the methods were used, to meeting and listening to some of the leaders of the sensitivity training and encounter groups, to reading a great deal of writing by them and about them. In addition to these sources of information, I have treated for many years persons who have problems similar to those persons who go to the sensitivity training and encounter group meetings. One of the reasons I have had for writing this book is that, as a psychiatrist and psychoanalyst, I have been aware in a special way of the problems and personalities of these people, of the difficulties involved in helping them, of the limitations of all the methods of treatment. It is with this background that I comment on the sensitivity phenomenon.

AN INVENTION
1 | OF OUR TIME

Sensitivity training and encounter has become very popular since its beginnings in New England twenty-five years ago. It has grown in the number and kinds of people who participate in its programs, in the many kinds of institutions which have sponsored and adopted it, in the diverse techniques and assorted theories which have been described under its name. The name refers to a proliferation of methods which attempt to cure every possible illness and to fulfill every conceivable need. It deals with serious issues of living and the serious problems of people, it attracts interest and raises the hopes of these people. It is necessary to examine it for these reasons, and also because it is not well defined and is poorly understood, because of its claims which are often extravagant, and because of the strong criticism directed at it.

Who goes to these sessions? It may seem that almost everybody goes. In fact, one of the leaders of the movement has written a book called: **Here Comes Everybody.**

The members of the student council of a high school spend a day at a "retreat"; the teachers in the school go to a weekend encounter. Parents bring children, often protesting and sullen children, to programs called "Seminars in Family Life"; married couples go off to "Marriage Encounters."

1

Corporation executives and their salesmen at the urging of the company participate in T-groups because the company believes that this participation will improve their administrative and leadership abilities, and so help business; sometimes the company brings the trainers into the home office or factory. Two years ago a book listed forty-one nationally known companies which have used these training methods. Policemen in Buffalo, Houston, New York City and other cities have been given sensitivity training so that they could better cope with the problems of crime and the ghetto. College students can receive academic credit for their participation in sensitivity training, and many colleges and universities list courses in these methods. Psychology 33 at the University of California at Davis includes two hours weekly of encounter; Social Relations 120 at Harvard is a course devoted to sensitivity training.

Two years ago sixty-five colleges and universities were in some way involved in sensitivity training. Included in the group were state and private universities, Catholic and nonsectarian colleges, undergraduate and graduate programs and colleges of medicine. Entire school systems have been influenced by sensitivity training and there are experimental projects in education using its methods and funded by organizations like the Ford Foundation. Two new colleges, Johnston College in California and Pima College in Arizona, have built their entire curriculum around the theories and techniques of sensitivity training and encounter. The Pan American Health Organization helped to develop a center in Chile. In other countries in South America, in countries in Asia, Africa, Australia and Europe there are sensitivity training programs.

Housewives, and unmarried women, and entire communities of nuns go to encounter sessions. So do artists, writers, welders, social workers, bartenders, college presidents, advertising men, bakers, perhaps even congressmen. Dropouts from school and society, users of drugs, people who have tried psychoanalysis and tranquilizers and bridge and religion are in the multitude of participants.

Some of these are healthy people who hope to know more about themselves, to express their feelings better, to have more satisfying relations with others. They have read in the literature sent out by the movement that they can grow and change, can realize their potential to the fullest, can gain a heightened self-awareness and an enjoyment of living. Many of the participants have been successful in their life and work; if young, they show promise of this success. They are well-educated, have friends, are loved. Others seek sensitivity training and encounter because they are unsure of themselves and believe they lack something important in their lives. They have not reached a personal fulfillment, or a sexual one, or an artistic one. They feel they lack purpose, closeness, freedom, accomplishments, independence, love. They are not manifestly disturbed or seriously depressed persons, but they are dissatisfied, unhappy, confused, lonely.

There are also persons who are emotionally ill and they come believing that they have finally found something to make them whole, or they have been advised to try it. Perhaps their psychiatrist has advised it, or their family doctor—even the American Academy of General Practice has been involved in the sensitivity training programs.

There is no selection from those who apply. The programs accept everyone who applies, and who can pay. It even advertises for customers. There are no carefully-laid-out precautions made for keeping out the depressed, the suicidal, the borderline or overtly psychotic person. These groups set forth no contra-indications to their procedures; they believe that sensitivity training and encounter is the treatment of choice (or the experience of choice, if you do not like the word treatment) for everybody.

In college and in high schools, in churches and in YMCA buildings, in business firms and in private homes, people are turning on. At this time there are thousands of these groups, some run by large organizations which have been doing it for a long time, and others are new, small and short-lived. The largest of these organizations is the National Training Laboratories Institute for Applied Behavioral Sciences, which has a staff of over five hundred psychiatrists, psychologists, sociologists and educators and which is planning to build in Virginia a university to conduct research in this field.

Jane Howard was a staff writer for *Life* magazine when she spent an entire year visiting sensitivity training programs and encounter groups and taking part in their programs. Even in this lengthy time she could visit no more than a handful of the centers. In 1968 when she gathered the material for her book, **Please Touch,** she listed eighty centers of various kinds, forty-five of them in California. San Francisco had nine, the largest number of any city.[1] Professor Donald H. Clark wrote that in August 1969 there were eighty-seven growth centers in the United States.[2] Miss Howard reported that twenty-five thousand people attend the Esalen Institute in Big Sur, California each year, and thousands more attend the sessions given by similar organizations that have sprung up in other cities, organizations with eye-catching names such as Kairos, Oasis, Espiritu, and Aureon. Dr. Irving Yalom wrote that in 1970 there were approximately two hundred sensitivity training and encounter groups in the Palo Alto, California area, and the Oakland, California branch of Synanon had fifteen hundred persons in its weekly group sessions, with another thousand persons on the waiting list.[3]

What is sensitivity training and encounter? The term covers many ideas and practices, some so different from the others that it is difficult to see how they can be thought of together. All of the programs have in common a group experience designed to encourage and provoke the revelation of feelings about one's self and about the other members of the group, feelings which one has often not been aware of, which have been repressed because they are painful. The group is usually small, rarely exceeding twenty, although there have been some sessions for audiences of several hundred persons. The experience itself is relatively brief, lasting from a few hours to a week or two in interrupted or in continuous (the so-called marathon) programs. It varies in intensity from meetings in which the participants discuss themselves in a superficial way and during which they may experience a moderate amount of anxiety, to encounters in which the participants attempt to get to "deep" feelings and may experience extreme emotional stress. Encounter is said to be concerned with the here-and-now, oriented to the real world of everyday existence, not concerned with the past as are psychoanalysis and psychotherapy. The focus is not on intellectual exchanges and understanding, but on experiencing, on the arousal of feelings through group interaction. "Respond," "React," are the bywords.

This group interaction may consist almost entirely of verbal exchanges, or it may include various kinds of physical contact. As the movement has spread it has relied more and more on physical and nonverbal methods. Often the interaction consists of what has been described as a "confrontation," that is, a frank, abrupt, often raw and violent interaction in which the usual social amenities are absent.

Miss Howard described sensitivity training and encounter in this way:

> An encounter group is a gathering, for a few hours, or a few days, of twelve or eighteen personable, responsible, certifiably normal and temporarily smelly people. Their destination is intimacy, trust, and awareness of why they behave as they do in groups; their vehicle is candor.[4]

I use the terms sensitivity training and encounter because they are the most widely used of the many terms current. There is not one distinct entity, but a potpourri, a collection that includes gestalt therapy, sensory awareness, bio-energetics, parapsychology, guided fantasy and dream trips, humanistic psychology, theater games, human potential movement, marathons. There are Nonverbal Labs, Conflict-Management Labs, and Risk-Taking Labs. It includes such improbable

names as the New Multi-Modal Methods of Nonverbal Communication, and Neo-Reichian Mini-Primals. It includes also
elements of psychodrama, Zen Buddhism, massage, meditation
and creative dance.
Miss Howard reported that:

> . . . . The movement is many things. It is a business, a means
> of recreation, a subculture, a counter-culture, a form of
> theatre, a philosophy of education, a kind of psychotherapy,
> and an underground religion with its own synods, sects,
> prophets, schisms, and heretics. Depending on who is
> assessing it, it is also a passing fad, a godsend, a silly collec-
> tion of parlor games, or a menace.[5]

What are the goals of sensitivity training and encounter?
What are the hopes of those who participate in it? Sensitivity
training began as an educational project, a way of learning how
people relate in groups and how group processes can change
people. These remain the goals of some programs, but others
see sensitivity training and encounter groups as a way of
reaching many other goals. These goals are much broader than
those the T-group leaders strive to attain, and they include
profound personality changes. Sensitivity training workshops
and encounter groups are advertised as events that enable persons to grow to fulfill their potentials; they are often advertised
as therapeutic. Some persons seek excitement and entertainment. These, too, are the goals of some of the leaders. Dr.
William Schutz has written a book called **Joy** and Dr. Alexander Lowen one called **Pleasure**. The sensory awareness and the
sensory awakening procedures are basically attempts to get the
maximum amount of pleasure from one's body.
Sensitivity training promises much. When the psychologist
Dr. Kurt Lewin and his associates began the T-groups, they
thought of them as enabling people to communicate better.
Sensitivity training is now seen by some enthusiasts as a way to
bring change to every area of living. Their programs promise to

help persons with all their problems of adjustment—emotional, scholastic, marital and many others. To know how important this promise is, one need only to count the numbers of personal advice columns in newspapers and magazines, take note of the popularity of books which deal with problems of adjustment and happiness, be aware of how many persons make their living by helping people with problems. Sensitivity training and encounter, its advocates claim, will have these results: people will shed their inhibitions, open themselves to their friends and families, even to strangers. Those who participate will have the courage to confront one another, to criticize and bring forth their long-buried feelings of resentment, jealousy, anger. These experiences will sharpen their senses, improve the tone of their muscles, lead them to greater awareness, to greater sexual arousal and intensify their pleasure. They will know themselves; they will feel more adequate. They will realize the fullness of their potential as feeling, creating, expressing, loving human beings.

This is the goal: to be able to live more fully. To experience more deeply. To find the answers to existence. Dr. William Schutz, one of the foremost encounter group leaders used the words from **Man of La Mancha** to express the hope that sensitivity training and encounter offers: "To dream the impossible dream . . . to reach the unreachable star." Many things are offered and those who promote this amazing, diverse collection of odds and ends of theory and practice claim each in his own way to cure all the ills, to make everyone more wonderful.

Those who are in this business are not at all modest in their claims. Dr. Carl Rogers, who popularized the encounter group, believes that it is "the most important social invention of our time." The Esalen Institute states that Esalen "represents a new approach to the family, medicine, the human body, sanity and madness, education, religion." One of the leaders of the movement, psychologist Dr. Abraham Maslow, said that Esalen was potentially one of the most important educational institutions in the world. In 1969 a Boston radio station present-

ed a racial confrontation called "T-group 15." Malcolm
Knowles, a professor at M.I.T., who is known as a human
relations expert, narrated the program and said it was:

> . . . the most profound experiment ever attempted in broad-
> casting . . . (and in the course of the confrontation the T-
> group members would) . . . tear at the roots of race,
> education, and personal communications, and in so doing lay
> bare many of the barriers built into each of us.[6]

Testimonials abound. Dr. Frederick Perls said his encounter
techniques would "make all individual therapy obsolete." Sensitivity has been called a "new world culture." The experiences
have been referred to as "transcendental" and "religious." The
writers publish the testimonials of those who have participated.
For example, Dr. Elizabeth Mintz writes that participants have
said:

> People are beautiful, and for the first time in my life I hope
> for happiness. . . . Today feels like the real beginning of my
> life. Today is my real birthday. . . . I was inside my skin, tight
> and alone. I never thought I'd use such language, it sounds
> corny, but now I feel related to the stars. . . . Never before
> did I feel so loved and accepted. . . . For the first time I am a
> part of all humanity.[7]

There is much advertising and salesmanship in all of this,
stirring up the needs and the anxieties, soliciting customers. It
seems to be the intent of many enthusiasts to convince people
they need it. The reason they need it is not because they are
mentally ill or have problems in adjusting to their lives, but
because everyone needs it. This is the human condition.

The theoretical framework for these programs, in so far as
they have a coherent framework, is a concept of human nature
which sees all persons as depressed, operating far below their
potential, but capable of experiencing and achieving a great

deal more than they do. Dr. Herbert Otto, who heads the National Center for the Exploration of Human Potential, in La Jolla, California, believes "healthy humanity is operating at ten to fifteen percent of its potential."[8] Human beings live in an environment which represses and constricts rather than stimulates, and they are denied those experiences which Otto and other writers say they are capable of having and are entitled to have. The environment of modern life restricts man's efforts instead of providing him with opportunities. Man is made fearful, ashamed, guilty, and so he does not venture. There is in this some of the philosophy of existentialism.

Sensitivity training is a growth experience. The movement is often called a growth movement, and its centers are growth centers. Some who write about sensitivity training and encounter claim it supplies what has, until now, been missing in human life. Since it is assumed that everyone can grow, and no one is making full use of his potential, then everyone is a candidate for their programs. Fitting in with this environmentalist view are the revisionist psychoanalytic theories of Fromm, May, Marcuse, and Norman O. Brown. In their view it is the culture that is unhealthy and the cause of illness and alienation, so the culture must be changed. The culture's repressions and facades operate through the legal, social, political and religious institutions, and these institutions must be changed or abandoned. The erosion of established authority is welcomed, and revolution is the expression of imagination, spontaneity, authenticity and togetherness.

Our modern civilization, say the sensitivity training and encounter exponents, alienates people. Our cities are filled with passive, fearful, inhibited people. Our lives are characterized by an absence of roots, a lack of intimacy, an identity diffusion, disillusionment, anomie, lack of relevance. Professor Clark says that the human race is "suffering from the malnutrition of misunderstanding and dying from a thirst we call alienation."[9] To those who believe this, sensitivity training and encounter appears to be the solution.

These group procedures are not considered to be group psychotherapy. Its leaders and followers say that it is educative, not therapeutic. At least they said it some years ago. However, there are now many who say there is a place for psychotherapy and that encountering augments psychotherapy. Then there are those who see no need for any therapy; psychotherapy and psychoanalysis are culture-bound, restrictive. The culture they impose on a person further alienates him. Some have accepted the ideas of British psychiatrist R.D. Laing and others who reject the concepts of mental illness and health.

Whether or not the leaders of the movement agree that there is mental illness, there are many emotionally ill persons who hope to find a cure in sensitivity training and encounter. They expect their personalities, their ways of perceiving themselves and the world, their bodily image, their attitudes and goals will be changed. These are the things unhappy, suffering people seek. The lonely, frightened, uncertain, depressed, confused—each one sees in the programs of the sensitivity movement a message of hope for himself. We need to ask if these hopes can be realized.

Some in the movement say that sensitivity training is treatment, that mentally ill persons do come and should come to their centers. Some, like Paul Bindrim, the originator of the nude marathon encounters, announce that they can help psychotic people and suicide-prone individuals. As a result of his nude marathons, "frigid females, impotent males and sexual exhibitionists have become at least temporarily free. Arthritics have been relieved of pain. Long-standing bachelors who could not commit themselves emotionally have married. Depressed individuals have been freed of suicidal tendencies. Psychotics in remission have lost their compulsive gestures and behaved normally by the end of a session."[10] Often they use the term "therapist" interchangeably with the term "leader" and create the impression that their programs are like group psychotherapy. They go further and say their programs offer better treatment than is offered in the mental hospitals and psychiatrists' offices. It is therapeutic, they say, because the participants really experience themselves; they live, they are in contact with reality. Bindrim claims his nude marathons enable those with distortions in their bodily images—and this includes a great many persons, sick and well—to correct these distortions when they see themselves and others without the disguise of clothing.[11]

Many questions have been raised about these programs and many persons have come forth to criticize their methods and goals. The list of critics includes the John Birch Society which views sensitivity training and encounter as subversive activity. One investigator of the movement wrote that in Los Angeles a person can dial a telephone message which tells him sensitivity training is a tool of the Communist conspiracy.[12] In 1969 a member of the House of Representatives had printed in The Congressional Record a lengthy attack on sensitivity training and related activities, comparing them to Communist brainwashing practices.[13]

Because of the extremist position of many of these critics it does not mean that all critics are under the influence of these paranoid outlooks. Responsible scientists, educators, clergy are concerned about the immediate and long-range effects of the programs, and have reason to be alarmed. There are also critics within the movement. Miss Howard wrote that many people in the movement cringe at the mention of the name of Paul Bindrim. Dr. Arthur Burton, a psychologist who conducts encounter groups, wrote:

. . . . Like all new growth movements it attracts the opportunist, the promoter, the self-styled leader, the charismatic would-be saint, the sick, and even the sadistic.[14]

He goes on to say that there is no follow-up of the effects of the group sessions, the dangers of sensitivity training are not acknowledged and the hurts inflicted by it have been ignored. Dr. Leonard Blank lists many kinds of misuse and abuse of sensitivity training and encounter, including

... the equivocal training of many group leaders; the questionable objectives of participants, as well as those who guide them; the problems of cultism and the buckshot application of group techniques; and the misapplication of these techniques.[15]

The priest-sociologist, Andrew Greeley, who is one of the more alarmed and perhaps intemperate critics and who is outside of the movement, writes that sensitivity training

... can be validated neither by psychoanalytic theory nor by proven empirical results. It is a dangerous, irresponsible, foolish practice, and the evangelical enthusiasm for it is not unlike the evangelical enthusiasm of the drug enthusiast.[16]

Of the many questions raised by these and other critics the most important are: Is this treatment? Are the theories on which these programs depend sound, validated, accepted by competent professionals? Who should be the leaders? What training should these leaders have? Who should participate? Should there be limitations on the behavior of the group members and the leaders?

Is it treatment? The concept of treatment contains many elements, and there are many ways of defining treatment depending on which of these elements are stressed. Two elements which include all of the others are the relationship between the therapist and the patient, and the techniques of treatment. The techniques often refer to the polarities of verbal as opposed to physical (drugs, electroshock, forms of restraint) and of supportive, directive and educational as opposed to nondirective and insight-producing. Some concepts of treatment are so broad that almost anything that is done with a person or said to him can be considered treatment. In this respect sensitivity training and encounter is treatment, for a treatment relationship occurs, at least in the widest sense of the term. An important part of these programs is their aim of intensifying the total personal contact of the group members with the leader and with one another. This is a relationship, but is it a helping relationship?

Those who write about these groups and those who lead them view traditional treatment relationships as limited and artificial. They assert that the group experience must provide a real-life relationship. In extreme situations the leader goes all the way to gain the participation of the group in words and actions dealing with all possible themes of living. One needs only to read the accounts of Dr. Perls' gestalt therapy, or of Dr. George Bach's marathons, to realize the lengths to which this is carried. Some think of the nude encounter groups where sex and aggression are openly encouraged as the ultimate in the therapeutic relationship. Others see them as an abandonment of the necessary social and emotional distance, not "real" in any sense, only thinly-disguised and rationalized acting out of impulses.

There are groups which offer training in leadership in industry, and industries such as the Polaroid Company, the Corning Glass Works, General Foods, and American Airlines which have sent their executives to these groups. There are other groups which aim to teach a more rewarding way of life to persons who are healthy, and these are the groups engaged in the growth movement. These are properly classified as belonging to business administration, to mental hygiene, or even to religion, but not to treatment programs. It is often difficult to know how far any of these programs go in the direction of treatment, and there are some of the interactions and techniques of all of these programs which belong in the realm of treatment and must be evaluated as such.

Treatment includes a responsibility for the welfare of those treated. If the sensitivity training and encounter methods are treatment, what steps are taken to safeguard those who participate in the groups? How reliable are the reports of psychotic reactions and other serious consequences? Regulatory bodies, licensing requirements and training standards are never an automatic and infallible protection for the patient, but they have been the best ways we know to weed out the incompetent and the charlatan. Evaluation of treatment methods and devices, even though it is imperfect, is the best way to prevent fraud and harm. For example, the "Product Information" required by the federal government for any drug on the market includes *description, actions, indications, contra-indications, warnings, precautions, adverse reactions* and *safe dosage* and *administration.* These are printed in the circular which the manufacturer must put into each package. There is no law which requires comparable information about psychotherapy and other drugless ways of helping persons who have emotional problems.

However, hospitals and clinics must meet standards of many state and federal regulatory bodies as well as those of professional organizations. There are licensing requirements for physicians, certification for clinical psychologists, accreditation for social workers. Patients have the opportunity for legal action in instances of malpractice, false advertising and unethical conduct. Sensitivity training and encounter has no means of regulation, no licensing of leaders, no standards, no standard-setting body. The only organization identified with sensitivity training is the American Institute of Humanistic Psychology, a forum for the views of the followers of Abraham Maslow and Carl Rogers and others of the "Third Force" in psychology, a group whose claims to professional and scientific competence are hardly accepted by the scientific community. Dr. Arthur Burton writes that many of the practitioners of sensitivity and encounter are persons who

. . . cannot meet the professional standards of clinical practice but nevertheless feel a calling to help people. A kind of anarchy takes over in which the leader with the greatest charisma, and the most diversified 'awakening' techniques, is the most desired and has the greatest following. Each leader builds a personal following by collecting testimonials and quickly forgets his obligation to science. While industry has set some standards for its human relations consultants, the broader exponents of encounter have not and do not promise to do so. I predict that in the decade ahead encounter leaders will require certification or license by the state once the evils have accumulated sufficiently to arouse public response.[17] What have the professional organizations said about these programs? In the September 27, 1971 issue of the *Journal of the American Medical Association*, the Council on Mental Health of this association emphasized that sensitivity training as such is not a recognized medical procedure and it is not identical with group or individual psychotherapy.[18] Both psychological benefits and psychological casualties have been reported, and among the casualties are depression, psychosis, major personality disorganization, anxiety reaction and homosexual panic. This report also describes the types of persons who are likely to have such reactions, and it lists safeguards relating to the qualifications of the leaders and the goals of the programs.

In 1970 the American Psychiatric Association published a Task Force report called: *Encounter Groups and Psychiatry*.[19] The chairman of the group which produced the report was Dr. Irvin Yalom, a psychiatrist from Stanford University who has had wide experience in group psychotherapy, in leading sensitivity training groups and in research studies on sensitivity training and encounter. The members of the study group were psychiatrists and psychologists well known for their work on groups. The group included Dr. Charles Seashore, a psychologist from the National Training Laboratories. This report emphasized the lack of data to substantiate the claims of benefits and harms from sensitivity training and encounter group sessions. The American Psychiatric Association took no stand on the programs other than to urge the psychiatrist, if he is involved in them, to fulfill his professional and ethical obligations to the participants. In 1971 and 1972 the research efforts of Dr. Yalom and his co-workers made an important beginning in supplying this needed research data.[20]

The periodical, *Psychology Today*, has reported favorably on many aspects of sensitivity training and encounter and has featured articles by and about the leaders of the movement. A recent issue had an interview with Dr. John Lilly, a psychiatrist who has become involved in Eastern mysticism and is one of the staff members of the Esalen Institute. He was interviewed by Sam Keen, a philosopher and a theologian who has also become a staff member of Esalen. The journal has interviewed Dr. Carl Rogers, Dr. Abraham Maslow, Mr. Michael Murphy, and others prominent in the movement. Many regard this journal as an authoritative source of scientific psychological information, just as some regard the periodical, *Voices,* as a valid source of information about psychotherapy; but, in fact, it may be surprising to some that these journals have no standing in the scientific community.

Questions must be asked about the assumptions underlying sensitivity training and encounter. Are the insights about human emotional life by which they are guided indeed verified, demonstrated knowledge, or are they only assumptions, or worse still, fantasies or myths? Some fantasies tend to reappear from time to time in scientific writings, especially those in social and psychological sciences. One is the fantasy of the infinitely perfectible man—a fantasy which fits in with the hopes of those in the Human Potential Movement. Another is that of the entirely conflict-free man, and it is hoped that this result can be attained by fashioning the conflictless environment. There is also the fantasy of the noble savage and the natural child free of anxiety and fears which those who advocate spontaneity and freedom of expression affirm. There is the mystique of spontaneity and the contention that feeling is the most reliable proof of truth. Add to these the assertion that the ultimate truth resides in the group.

In times past, these myths, having been applied in the social and political arenas, have found expression in religion. They are not new, but mostly a renaming of old ideas. The leaders of sensitivity training and encounter like to think they are breaking new ground, discovering new truths and leading to the promised land; but, whether or not they are aware of it, they are usually presenting ideas which have been discarded by responsible scientists. The ideas of Perls, Goodman, Schutz and Lowen were proposed by the dissidents from classical psychoanalysis forty and fifty years ago, by Adler, Rank, Reich, Ferenczi and Horney.

An example of these assumptions is the thesis of the gestalt therapists that spontaneity is essential. In the book **The Making of a Counter Culture**, Theodore Roszak writes:

> . . . The behavior of children, heroes, lovers, 'simple folk,' and people in crisis is beautiful and ethically inspiring . . . (it is) a mystical psychology whose conception of human nature sides aesthetically with the non-intellective spontaneity of children and primitives, artists and lovers, who lose themselves gracefully in the splendor of the moment.[21]

In addition, there are assumptions about psychology which are still debatable, and which concern matters of such importance that the open-minded investigator should take the trouble to find out what has been said on both sides. There have been and continue to be men of great ability and profound understanding who have studied these problems, have devoted their lives to advancing our knowledge of the human mind, to finding ways of living which will bring about mental health, and ways to treat those who suffer from mental illnesses and emotional disturbances. Throughout the writings on sensitivity training and encounter are attacks on these scholars and practitioners. Dr. Arthur Burton in his introductory chapter to his book, **Encounter**, contends that psychoanalysis and psychotherapy have failed to solve the human problems and that encounter is their successor.[22] In the view of some of the disciples of the movement, anyone whose practice is guided by traditional psychological theories, especially by psychoanalytic theory, is by that fact biased and unable to evaluate the sensitivity phenomenon.

It is difficult to see how there can be agreement on theory supporting a movement which includes yoga, massage, nude marathons, arm and thumb wrestling, meditation, existentialism, poetry, the "Rational-Emotive" treatment of Dr. Albert Ellis, gestalt therapy, transactional analysis and many others. There seem to be some common denominators, although not all agree on even these few things. Let your feelings be your guide, do it in the here and now, listen to the group feedback, respond and react, don't analyze. For sensitivity training and encounter groups these are the most reliable guides to reality and to truth. One writer tells how the group brings about what he calls "reality testing":

> . . . An important activity of the therapist. . . . is to force the client to verbalize expectations, his own self-condemnations, the group's responses, particularly to hear the latter. The therapist may insist that the client ask group members how they feel about him, that he perceive the discrepancy, that he take the group seriously.[23]

In other words, the judgment of the group is the basis of reality. The contention is that people do not need insight, that it is not necessary that one understand his conflicts. It is superfluous to dig back into the past to uncover the sources of emotional difficulties. The here-and-now group interaction will tell a person all he needs to know about himself.

Yet there appears to be a contradiction in that some of the leaders feel it is necessary for the group to regress to the time of childhood, and to this end the participants are caressed, rocked, wrestled, given nursing bottles, encouraged to recall traumatic childhood experiences and to relive them. Although the person's early life is said not to be important, the encounter will make things right by making up for the deficiencies of love and sensory gratification in early life. This is only one of the many contradictions which those in the movement ignore.

Feelings are the most reliable guide to honesty and to authenticity. Repression of feelings is dishonest. It is putting on armor, assuming masks, playing roles. The theories of sensitivity training and encounter assign an absolute value to feelings, and they measure everything else by feeling. Rational, cognitive methods and goals have no place in their scheme. It is good if it feels good; it is right if it feels right. Religion is a feeling, and peak experiences are religious feelings. Values and morality, the standards and fabric of society, must be evaluated in terms of feelings. The group consensus is the final judge of everything. As much as the advocates of these exercises proclaim that they liberate the individual, give him autonomy, what they liberate him from is all control over his feelings. Inner control of every kind they seem to regard as repressive, as they do external control. They do not take into account that in their scheme the individual is not liberated from the pressures and coercion of the group.

What are the results of the regressions which these groups produce? Are they dangerous? Professor Clark writes that he has heard only rumors of persons being damaged, rumors which he found difficult to confirm.[24] I know of actual instances of damage to people who have been in encounter groups, persons who have required hospitalization. Others who have studied the movement have reported these tragedies. Some of the leaders of the groups admit that psychotic breaks and other casualties have occurred, but they dismiss them by saying that they were going to happen anyway. This appears to be a particularly insensitive way of dealing with peoples' emotions. Although many of them claim their methods are superior to traditional therapies and they can help depressed persons—psychotic and suicidal persons, as well as those with neurotic symptoms and character disorders—they are not willing to take the responsibility which professionals take. Professor Clark writes:

. . . Perhaps one day we shall be free of the medical model of responsibility and the customer will be aware that he is solely responsible for his own growth whether it is stimulated by exploration, instruction, or psychotherapy.[25]

Bindrim takes care to see that his nude marathons violate none of the laws of the community where they are held, and he requires the participants to sign a "legal" contract before they take part in his encounters. He may feel that in this way he is discharging his responsibility to them, but his concern seems to be only with the laws and with the external conformity to these laws.

Finally, what are the long-term results? What proof, aside from testimonials, do we have that sensitivity training and encounter produce the benefits that are promised? Some feel there is no need to evaluate the procedures, yet claim that these groups produce more meaningful education, more genuine relationships, more truth, more honesty in living. By what means do they measure these things?

It is important to evaluate these procedures. Why should a parent permit his child to attend a free university or one of the new colleges modelled entirely on the procedures of encounter? Can he find some way, other than the testimonials, to know if this education is superior to that of a recognized, accredited university which has produced generations of educated persons? How can a psychiatrist or a guidance counselor or a clergyman know that he is helping a person who comes to him when he sends that person to an encounter group? What evidence other than the claims of the promoters do we have that the movement will produce better educated, more creative, less neurotic people? Are encounter experiences genuine growth experiences as the advocates claim? Do they lead to creativity and discovery? What have they created and discovered that we do not already know? Do they encourage people to live out sick fantasies and impulses and call this creative? Does it really beg the question to say that being one's self and doing one's thing results in overthrowing hypocrisy, in finding truth? Is the phenomenon of sensitivity oversimplified, manipulative, coercive, a parody of life, of relationships, of love, of intimacy?

There are benefits from sensitivity training and encounter, although they are difficult to measure. There are responsible persons in the movement. There are valid criticisms of our social institutions and of the ways of living which produce emotional disorders and keep people from using their gifts. Somehow the responsible leaders and investigators do not get the attention that the extremists and the cultists get. In raising the questions which I have raised and in attempting to answer them, I am not taking the position that sensitivity training and encounter has no value.

Beginnings of the
2 | Group Movement

Sensitivity training and encounter did not develop within a scientific discipline as psychoanalysis developed within the field of medicine and behaviorism within the field of psychology. The history of the movement is the history of many things, cultural, political, scientific, educational and religious. It is part of, and a response to, some of the social and political changes that have occurred in this country since the end of World War II, and especially since 1960. Some of the goals of the reformers in social and political causes have become the goals of the persons who are identified with the sensitivity movement, and many persons in the movement are active in liberal and even radical causes.

The history of the movement touches on the struggles over civil rights, the Vietnam war and the draft, student revolt. It includes changes in theology, from the death of God movement to the breakdown in barriers to interfaith cooperation, and the attempts to reform outmoded religious forms of administration and worship. Changes have taken place in education, in leisure-time activities, in the fashions of dress, changes that have been mostly in the direction of a loosening of restrictions and adopting of more permissive attitudes.

Until recently, the philosophy of most people in this country, the so-called American way of life, emphasized a reasonable, traditional style of living which was based, at least in principle if not always in practice, on adherence to an accepted morality, on a practical and materially-oriented viewpoint on work, personal relationships and recreation. This could be seen in the reverence many had for the large and influential organizations in business and government, and in their willingness to work in these organizations. It was seen in the respectability with which the people endowed these organizations.

In these years there were grave social injustices, but few critics. There were few who opposed the established order, and those who did attracted little notice, or if they were noticed were considered bizarre and influenced few people. Those who fought for reforms in the treatment of Negroes had little success until the middle of the 1950s. Those who advocated radical departure from accepted practice and from accepted doctrine in the churches were controlled through censorship, and the radicals in politics, at least those of the left, were subdued by the excesses of the Senator Joseph McCarthy era.

Before 1960, little attention was paid outside of some professional circles to the sociological and psychological studies which led to sensitivity training and encounter. These studies had been in progress for a long time, especially the studies concerned with group processes. By the late 1940s, some important contributions had been published, and in the 1950s industry became interested in the knowledge and techniques of group dynamics. By the 1960s, the avant-garde and extremists had caught on to the trend. This was the birth of the sensitivity phenomenon proper.

Many things changed in the 1960s and many questioned long-cherished values. The sensitivity phenomenon offered answers to some questions, attempted to fill the void left when the cultural institutions that had provided some stability and intimacy became weakened. People were receptive to the promises given by psychedelic drugs, return to nature, mystical religions and many other things, including sensitivity training. The "openness" of those in the movement is nowhere more apparent than in their willingness to accept into their schemes almost anything in the way of technique and almost any theory. The history of the movement can start almost anywhere, with almost anything. This is why it is difficult to trace in an orderly way the history of its development. For many persons sensitivity training and encounter encompasses all of the important matters of life—religious, scientific, aesthetic, moral. The history of its development includes all of these.

One could begin as far back as the fifth century before Christ when Gotama Buddha lived in India and taught a religious way of life which has found expression in many countries and cultures. The followers of Buddha seek an inner freedom, a tranquility of spirit, a transcendence of the limitations of existence. To do away with sufferings, men must do away with the cravings that cause these sufferings. One of the many contradictions of the sensitivity movement is that it can accept the sensuality that is so much a part of the methods advocated by Gunther, Bindrim and others at the same time that it accepts the mortification of the senses that is part of Buddhism. However, those in the movement do not see a contradiction for in both instances a more intense experiencing is sought, and experiencing is central to the concept of sensitivity training and encounter.

One could go back to the sixteenth century when the Indians of Mexico used the cactus *peyote* to bring about changes in their sense perceptions. At least four centuries ago it was known that this alkaloid could produce visual and auditory hallucinations, could result in acute perceptions of sounds and sights, and a feeling of levitation. Today these are considered to be manifestations of toxicity or of impaired mental functioning, but the peyote users thought them to be religious phenomena. Tribes south of the Rio Grande River soon became users of the drug and Peyotism was practiced as a religious cult, the drug being used in ritual manner to cure sickness, lessen hunger and fatigue and produce states of ecstasy. In modern times the Plains Indians have added elements of the white man's christianity to their traditional drug cult to form a new religion. Called "The Native American Church of the United States," it has given to the quarter million Indians who are its adherents a messianic, mystical and evangelical way of life that has filled the void in their existence resulting from the white man's civilization. It is to be remembered in relation to this that Dr. Timothy Leary proclaimed his drug cult as a new religion.

We could go to the year 1778, the year Anton Mesmer arrived in Paris, having hastily left his native Vienna. The discoverer of "animal magnetism" was acclaimed by the people of Paris as he worked his wonders on individuals and on groups, on the sick and on the healthy. The metal rods and other paraphernalia he used had no special powers, and his results were due to the suggestibility, the wishful thinking of the populace. Yet, by his techniques, Mesmer provoked in persons attacks of emotional and physical outbursts, laughing, crying, contortions, even psychic phenomena such as clairvoyance. Mesmerism was in vogue in Europe and in England for more than a half century, and was hailed as a great boon to humanity. Some of the manifestations of encounter are not unlike the marvels Mesmer wrought, and many of the leaders of today's movement have their devoted followers just as Mesmer did. It is also to be noted that many of those who belong to religious sects, particularly those of the pentecostal variety, lean heavily on emotional expressions and manifestations of the spirit, and their manifestations are similar to the hysterical reactions of Mesmer's followers.

The movement known as Moral Rearmament also was a forerunner of sensitivity training and encounter. Beginning in 1902, Frank Buchman brought an evangelistic ministry to the youth in seminaries and colleges in the Eastern part of the United States. Although Buchman's movement had a definite religious message and a moral absolutism, it contained many of the features we find today in the sensitivity movement. Most of the activity took place in conferences, or "house parties," which emphasized candor, honesty and mutual respect among the participants. Personal testimony, or "witnessing," came to be an important part of the house parties. When Buchman, at his first house party, felt impelled to confess a minor wrongdoing, he feared the reaction of the group would be unfavorable. To his great surprise, he found he had started a chain of confessions that affected not only those present at the house party, but the future course of the movement. From that time the testimony became an essential part of its group method.

Buchman persuaded labor leaders and industralists to attend his house parties, and this was a forerunner of the involvement of Lewin and his co-workers with industry. Buchman also worked with racial problems and alcoholics, and had some influence in founding Alcoholics Anonymous, which through its offshoot, Synanon, is related to the sensitivity training and encounter movement.

Buchman believed these groups were effective because they separated persons from their regular pursuits for a time and gave them an opportunity to consider religion and their own particular religious experiences. In this informal setting a more intimate contact was possible. Buchman's movement reached, as does the sensitivity training and encounter movement, the middle class rather than the poor or the wealthy. It is important to keep in mind, I think, that although sensitivity training and encounter leaders have been so critical of our society and its abuses, although they emphasize a humanistic outlook, they do not seem concerned with remedying the problems of social welfare, of political oppression, of social injustices.

During the nineteenth century, several groups in this country attempted to live a communal life and stressed this self-revelation. The Amana colonies had their *untersuchen*, or mutual confession. At the Oneida community, founded in 1844 in New York State, there were sessions in which the entire community censured or praised a person for his actions. Later the political groups, such as the Marxist-Leninists, held what they called "consciousness-raising" sessions.

Religious beliefs, drug cults and fads are not the only sources of the sensitivity movement. It has a connection with the behavioral sciences and many of its leaders have doctoral degrees in these sciences. The specifically scientific origins are from two main sources: the researches of social psychology, particularly the psychology and sociology of small groups, and the practice of psychotherapy.

The important theories of group behavior which are related to sensitivity training and encounter are these: (1) The group influences the behavior, changes the attitudes of its members and leads them to a consensus. (2) It does these things by enabling the members to be aware of each other's feelings and experiences, and by collective problem solving. (3) The group can solve certain problems more effectively than the individual, it is claimed, because the individual working alone is often unable to overcome his blind spots, or in the language of group dynamics, his habitual "learning sets," and so he cannot effectively and objectively evaluate his own ideas. (4) Because the group is made up of interacting individuals, there is necessarily conflict in groups. The conflict need not lead to the break-up of the group but can result in learning, integration and problem solving. (5) The face-to-face contact with one another, the necessary frankness and self-revelation in the group, enables the individuals in it to experience vicariously the feelings and conflicts of each other, and so to identify in varying degrees with one another.

Individuals interacting in a group exist for each other in a psychological fashion, and respond to each others' feelings, actions and experiences. It should be kept in mind, and we will consider this more fully later, that this is not limited to groups, for it happens also in a two-person relationship, where only one of the two, the patient, reveals himself.

Dr. Kurt Lewin has rightfully received credit for clarifying important elements of group behavior, and his studies led to group dynamics and to sensitivity training and encounter. Yet, all of the above characteristics of small groups were described before Lewin's researches, during a period from 1880 to 1910 by the sociologists Ferdinand Tonnies, Lester Ward, George Simmel and Charles Cooley. Lewin's work on field dynamics, or the influence of groups, was published in Germany in the 1920s. When he came to the United States he worked at the University of Iowa and was able to test experimentally his hypotheses concerning groups. An important study dealt with the differences between groups which were structured in authoritarian fashion as opposed to those structured in either a democratic or a laissez-faire fashion. His classic experiments showed that the members of the authoritarian group, in contrast to the members of the other two groups, lacked initiative and independence, were more hostile, aggressive, frustrated and self-centered.

Before Lewin, some writers supposed that the actions of the group were the result of something called the "group mind." This view did not take into account the importance of the individual and it was not until Lewin's theories that the individual was related to the group in a meaningful way. Lewin's theories were of particular importance because they resolved some problems in conceptualizing the relationship of the individual to the group and made it possible to understand both the group and the individual acting in the group. His basic viewpoint is that the characteristics of the group come from the characteristics of its members and from the dynamic relations which the individuals have to one another. There is a continuous process of adaptation of the members to one another and to the problem each one presents.

Lewin's concepts, and those of his predecessors, were about psychological groups, that is, small, face-to-face groups of interacting individuals. In this group each individual has enough awareness of the others so that they are able to interact. The psychological group forms a *field*, a term used to describe group behavior as a whole, and this field, this psychological group structure, is the decisive factor in the behavior of each person in the group.

The importance of Lewin's concepts was that they did away with the necessity to explain the group behavior in terms of superimposed ideas such as the group mind, or a mystical, charismatic quality of the leader to which the group members respond. Group behavior can be understood by studying the relationships between the individuals of the group; the leadership can be explained in terms of a reciprocal relationship between the leader and the group members. If the leader is a so-called charismatic leader, for example, this alone will not explain his acceptance by the group; he is accepted only if the group members wish such a leader.

Lewin was the first to use the term "group dynamics," and his work led to the large-scale application of the principles of group dynamics to industrial relations and to the problems of community relationships. However, his was not the first study of industrial problems, nor the first experimentation in that area. In the late 1920s, the sociologist, Elton Mayo, urged that social-psychological concepts be applied to industry, and in the late 1930s, Roethlesberger and Dickson applied Mayo's principles in their investigations of the Western Electric Company's Hawthorne plant in Chicago. We have mentioned Buchman's work with labor and industry leaders. Lewin was able to demonstrate that the problems of workers in industry could be lessened if the management paid attention to group processes. When individuals in a group were able to participate in the gathering of information about their problems and were able to take part in solving these problems, they accepted the solutions. They accepted them because they had gathered the facts and had come to the conclusions. The facts and conclusions were the result of their own group processes and had not been imposed on them in an authoritarian way. They trusted the group because they trusted themselves. Lewin also saw his methods as valuable tools for the understanding of cultural, economic, sociological and psychological factors of group life, for assessing the problems of planned social change and of resistance to change. He felt that group procedures could be effective in changing attitudes and conduct.

An important assertion of field theory is that interdependence is always present in groups. All part of a life space, all parts of a field, are interdependent. This is closely related to the theory of the gestalt. Another basic tenet of Lewin's theory is the "principal of contemporaneity of causation," which means that at any given time the only things which determine the behavior of the parts of a field are the properties of the field *at that time.* This principle has been misunderstood and taken to mean that Lewin did not understand the importance of early life experiences for personality development. Those in sensitivity training and encounter who say that we must deal only with the here-and-now and not deal with the past, are mistaken if they claim Lewin as their authority. Some believe that Lewin's data refute the genetic hypothesis which holds that early developmental stages influence the course of later development. It was also felt that Lewin held learning as unimportant. Lewin did not attack the genetic hypothesis of the psychoanalytic theory, nor did he diminish the importance of learning. He valued both, and in his writings emphasized the importance of obtaining a history of a person's life in order to determine his present state. He wrote in some detail about the problems and methods of conducting research on group culture and history. There are those in the sensitivity training and encounter movement who assert that diagnosis and life history have no value, but they cannot rightfully claim Lewin as the source of these views.

Group psychotherapy, or the treatment of emotionally ill persons in groups, is another source of sensitivity training and encounter. Group psychotherapy developed from the understanding of normal and abnormal psychology of the individual as well as from the knowledge of normal and abnormal psychology of social groups. Individuals in groups manifest reactions and symptoms like those of persons with emotional problems, and the group interaction often leads to the resolution of the tensions and conflicts of the group. It was felt that in group psychotherapy an individual's psychological health could be restored.

Group psychotherapy, like group dynamics, is not new. Freud called attention to the importance of group behavior and the interrelatedness of the individual to others and to groups, although he did not develop a theory or technique of group psychotherapy as such.

More than forty years ago, an American psychiatrist, Dr. Trigant Burrow, brought forth the idea that if the person who has a distorted self-image was placed in a social situation where he could see himself as he is and be accepted by others his neurotic self-image could be corrected. Dr. Burrow felt that emotional illness was a disturbance in communication, based on the patient's "privately cherished and secretly guarded" image of himself. People can get well, he felt, by expressing themselves as they really are. The openness of the sensitivity training and encounter groups is nothing new.

Even earlier than this was the work of the Viennese psychiatrist, Dr. Jacob Moreno. A few years before the turn of the century he organized some prostitutes of Vienna into groups which met at coffee houses to discuss their difficulties, and from his experiences in helping these persons he eventually fashioned a technique of group psychotherapy known today as psychodrama. Dr. Moreno felt that the person who had internal tensions and conflicts could obtain relief by acting out these conflicts on the stage, by releasing these tensions in a group drama. He used staff members and other patients whom he called "auxiliary egos" to aid the patient in expressing his feelings. For years Dr. Moreno's institution in Beacon, New York has been a center where many persons have been trained in this type of group therapy. Many of the early papers of the social scientists who developed group dynamics were published in the journals of the Moreno Institute. Although Dr. Moreno thought of this psychodrama as spontaneous group processes, they were partly structured by the group leaders. The same observation might be made of many of the encounters and confrontations which are called spontaneous, but are, in fact, directed and structured by experienced group leaders.

In 1905, Dr. Joseph Pratt, an American physician, attempted to cure people with tuberculosis by bringing them together in groups. At the Massachusetts General Hospital he introduced his "class method" in order to help his tubercular patients adhere more consistently to the rules of diet and hygiene which were so important to their recovery. Through these classes they discovered that persons in peer groups can help one another. Dr. Pratt felt that a patient's emotional state influenced the course of his disease and he observed that tubercular patients tended to become isolated and depressed. His treatment method also included home visits and weekly meetings of the patient groups during which the events of their daily lives were discussed.

One of the early psychoanalysts, Dr. Alfred Adler, used group methods with members of the working class, and Dr. E.W. Lazelle in the first decade of this century worked with groups of schizophrenic patients at St. Elizabeth's Hospital in Washington, D.C. Dr. L. Wender in the 1930s worked with hospitalized patients who were not psychotic. Dr. Paul Schilder and Mr. Samuel Slavson are others in those early years who used group methods to treat patients.

Sensitivity training and encounter may appear similar to group psychotherapy, and some in the sensitivity movement do not make a distinction between their methods and those of group psychotherapy. To understand how group psychotherapy differs from the methods of sensitivity training and encounter, it is important to look at some of the important characteristics of group psychotherapy. Group psychotherapy contradicts none of the basic principles of group dynamics, since sick persons behave in groups according to the same principles that govern the behavior of healthy persons. Group psychotherapy is not a substitute for individual psychotherapy. It is not superior to it, nor does it necessarily take less than individual treatment.

Both individual and group therapy are verbal therapies, although in some forms the group members use role playing as a means of expressing feelings and conflicts. Aside from this, the patient communicates and makes relationships in treatment through the use of words. Sensitivity training and encounter groups make a greater use of nonverbal and active methods.

The advocates of sensitivity training, and encounter speak of their methods as being permissive, and so do the therapists who treat individuals and groups. But they often use the word to mean different things. Permissive, used in psychotherapy, means that the patient is free to say any of his thoughts or feelings and he will not be censured or judged because he has spoken these thoughts and feelings. Permissive in the context of psychotherapy means that thoughts and feelings can be expressed; it does not extend to the acting out of these feelings, and the patient is expected to control his urges to express his feelings in action. The therapist in individual and group psychotherapy is granted less of this permissiveness than is the patient. He does not, except when it is indicated on strictly technical grounds, give his personal reactions to the patient and to what the patient says; he does not act on his feelings.

Openness in psychotherapy has been valued highly, and rightly so, but this openness is not an end in itself. People experience a relief when they are able to say something which they have been ashamed to talk about, or when they have expressed emotions which they had kept to themselves. The relief from this catharsis is usually brief, and it is often followed by guilty or anxious feelings. Patients are encouraged to say things because this is the first step in understanding themselves, in clarifying their thinking, in correcting misapprehensions, in assessing their relationships with others. The openness itself is not so desirable that the therapist does not respect the patient's resistance to saying all of his thoughts and feelings. The good therapist and leader knows the importance of these resistances; he attempts to help the patient to understand their meaning so that he can overcome them.

The therapist does not force the patient to break through these resistances.

For group therapy to have any success and meaning, the individual must maintain his own identity and self-respect—indeed, it is important that these are strengthened through the group's acceptance of him as an individual. Unless this occurs, the group takes on the characteristics of the crowd in which the individual's identity and worth are lost.

Unlike groups such as community relations groups, the therapeutic group is not directed toward group goals, except in the very general sense of promoting the health of the group, but it is directed toward the health of each individual member. Groups for treatment are constituted in such a way that all of the individuals in them will benefit. Enough must be known of each patient selected for a group that the group leader can be confident that the patient's contributions and interactions will not break up the group and increase the pathology of the individuals in it. Although some do not like the terminology, this means that members are selected for the therapy groups through the processes of evaluation and diagnosis.

The therapist is an important person in the therapeutic group, so important that I do not believe there can truly be a leaderless group. Some person, or at times several persons, will become, in fact, the leader of such groups. Knowledge of individual psychotherapy does not necessarily make one a capable group psychotherapist, for the therapist needs also an understanding of group processes. The group leader or therapist does structure the group, but does not impose his own ideas on the group, just as the individual therapist does not impose his views of life on his patients. The therapist's goal is to permit the group processes to operate freely with a minimum of interference. Part of the reason group therapy works is because, if the group is properly constituted, the patient recognizes that despite his limitations and difficulties he is accepted by the group. This support helps him to regain his self-esteem, makes him feel able to relate to others, increases his confidence in himself and his trust in others.

All groups are therapeutic in some degree, and this includes problem-solving groups. In any group, a person finds emotional fulfillment and a satisfaction of his needs. Therefore, some persons in sensitivity training and encounter think that there is no real distinction between therapy groups and other groups. Statements such as the one by Dr. Carl Rogers to the effect that the same processes that make sick people well make well people better, are taken to mean that there is really no difference in the groups, that no special training or qualifications are needed to work with groups of sick persons.

Sensitivity training and encounter differs from group psychotherapy in almost all of the things I have listed. It does not require or advocate training, the leaders are forceful, directive and interfering. Openness and frankness are ends in themselves. Resistances, which they call facades or masks, must be done away with. The leaders do not set limits on their own interaction with the group members and permit or encourage this interaction, putting thoughts into actions rather than restricting them to words. They do not ask if certain persons do not belong in their groups, or if they would be harmed by particular methods. The practice of this type of sensitivity training and encounter has been labelled a "shotgun" approach.

A third scientific source of the sensitivity phenomenon is the work of Dr. Wilfred Bion of England in group processes. His work stands somewhere between the group dynamics approach and the group psychotherapy methods. Bion's theories were based on small therapy groups he worked with at the Tavistock Clinic in London and on his study of large social groups such as the army and the church. In these latter settings he studied aspects of group behavior such as the psychology of mob rule and the methods by which a group selects its leaders. Dr. Bion's work was introduced into the United States by Dr. Margaret Rioch of Washington in a paper she delivered in 1965 to the Mid-Atlantic Group Psychotherapy Society.

Bion's contribution to the understanding of group psychology can be best approached by describing his classification of groups. There are two types of groups: (1) those which function on the basis of the task to be accomplished, and (2) those groups which function on the basis of the emotional needs of their members. These are called, respectively, the "work groups" and the "basic assumption" groups. They are not exclusive of each other, and any existing group has in it aspects of both the work and the basic assumption groups. The work group is similar to the problem-solving groups of Lewin and others. Bion uses the term *basic assumption* to mean that the emotional relationships of the participants to one another and to reality are *based* on certain *assumptions* about themselves and reality. They behave as though these assumptions were true. For example, before Columbus discovered America, sailors believed that the earth was flat. Because of this assumption they did not sail far from the coast, believing that they might fall off the edge of the earth. In like manner, the group members behave as if their basic assumptions about themselves and the other members of the group and the world, usually tacit or even unconscious assumptions, were true. While the work group is reality oriented, the basic assumption group is oriented toward fantasies which the group may impulsively and uncritically carry out.

Bion described three types of basic assumption groups: dependency, fight-flight and pairing. The dependency group looks to a powerful and wise leader for protection and help; it is exemplified in the familiar doctor-patient relationship. The fight-flight group is one which feels threatened and can preserve itself only by fighting the thing or person threatening it, or by running away. This group usually has a strong anti-intellectual bias, needs the kind of leader who sees everything in terms of attacking or being attacked, and one who can mobilize the group to action. Political and religious organizations which are extreme in their views, with a fanatical dedication and a paranoid kind of thinking, are examples of these groups. The pairing group operates through two persons who it hopes will produce for the rest of the group the program or individuals which will fulfill their hopes. In the fight-flight and the pairing groups there is also the element of dependency.

Bion distinguished between group psychotherapy properly conceived and that which he called psychotherapy "done in public." By this latter he refers to the treatment of an individual in the presence of the group, a device in which the individual group members may take turns being the patient while the rest of the group functions as co-therapists. This is what Dr. Frederick Perls used in the methods he called gestalt therapy. Bion does not consider the use of these methods to be a proper use of the group's potentials for therapeutic change.

In Bion's view, group methods help the individual to accomplish specific goals and do certain work. They are not vehicles to bring to the members great love and overwhelming warmth, a sense of cosmic transcendence and unity. Togetherness is not a goal of the group processes; that people seek togetherness in groups, Bion feels, is a defense against the fear of being alone or having to work alone. Those who lead groups patterned after Bion's concepts of group interaction do not seek the intense experiencing, the self-revelation and self-exploration, do not search for deep intimacy and do not look for those peak experiences and moments of ecstasy which many of the sensitivity groups seek.

Bion's work on groups is represented in this country by the "Group Relations Conferences" which are frequently held in the Eastern part of the United States. These groups are structured and make limited use of techniques other than verbal ones. Bion's followers constitute what has been termed the "right wing" of the movement. This is in contrast to the "left wing" exemplified by the unstructured and eclectic approach of Esalen.

Lewin's concepts and his experiments became a movement in 1946. They might never have become known beyond academic halls and scientific laboratories were it not for a fortuitous event. Connecticut had recently enacted a fair-employment-practices law, and the director of the Connecticut Interracial Commission, disturbed by some anti-semitic incidents, asked Dr. Lewin's help in training persons to implement the law and to deal with interracial tensions. At the State Teachers College in New Britain, Connecticut, Lewin and his associates conducted a workshop in which small groups discussed the community problems which the members presented to them. A research observer was part of each group and his task was to record the interactions of the group members. The observers met each night with the leaders to share their reports with them. Some of the group members learned of these meetings and asked if they could attend. The leaders reluctantly consented, and, as Benne wrote, their effect on the group was "electric." The group members responded to and reacted to the research observers' reports of their behavior in the group, and thus was born the technique which became specific for the T-groups. The members of the group would be confronted with the observations of their behavior and its effects on others, and they would be expected to respond to this information. In this way, the members learned more of how they acted in a group; in this way another level of group interaction was introduced.

The following year, three of Dr. Lewin's associates, Drs. Leland Bradford, Ronald Lippit and Kenneth Benne began the training laboratories at the Gould Academy in Bethel, Maine. These were called "basic skill training groups," a designation that was later shortened to "T-groups." From the modest enrollment of sixty-seven that first year, the programs have grown to where they train more than twenty-five hundred leaders each year. In 1950, the National Training Laboratory was established as a year-round training program as part of the National Educational Association. From the beginning it was emphasized by the NTL that it offered training in human relations, not in psychotherapy.

In the years that followed, the emphasis of the T-groups changed, and for many of them the interpersonal behavior of the group members became the focus of the group activity. The movement spread to the West Coast. At UCLA, an Institute of Industrial Relations was established to study the potentials of the T-group for industry. The Western Training Laboratories coined the term "sensitivity training" to describe its programs for making people more effective managers and leaders. In 1959, the Western Behavior Sciences Institute was opened at La Jolla, California. All of the above considered themselves to be professional, scientific organizations dedicated to applying the findings of group dynamics to various fields, especially to industry and education. Although these organizations emphasized individual growth more than the parent groups on the East Coast, they were begun as serious scientific groups.

Of a different sort are the groups which began in the 1960s, mostly on the West Coast. The Esalen Institute is perhaps the best known of these. The groups used as one base for their programs the interactions of the T-groups, but they made changes which produced confrontations and exchanges of a much different kind. They went beyond the goal of training the members in group processes, and endeavored to change human beings in all ways, physically, psychologically, socially, spiritually. It has been said that the difference between the NTL type of sensitivity training and the Esalen type is that the former train and that the latter do psychotherapy. There is some truth in this, but the Esalen type of group attempts to do more than psychotherapy ever attempts to do. Except for those therapists who practice the most directive and authoritarian type of therapy, as is the case with Dr. Albert Ellis and his Rational-Emotive Therapy, therapists usually do not have such grandiose expectations of what they can accomplish. While some of the leaders of the growth groups call their collection of methods psychotherapy, this does not mean that they offer treatment in any accepted sense of the word.

Esalen and its offspring and imitators seem to have been created solely for the "enhancement of human development," a term which is elastic enough to cover all of its programs. A brochure was published advertising an Esalen "East Coast

Weekend" in 1971, and this described Esalen as "a center to explore those trends in the behavioral sciences, religion and philosophy, which emphasize the potentialities and values of human existence." The weekend offered, in addition to the usual kinds of encounters, seminars and workshops on "Psychic Healing," on "The Inevitable Transformation of Mankind," on "The Alexander Technique," on "Continuous Satori-Samadhi," on "The Psychology of Meditation," and others. It also offered a Sunday morning "Aquarian Age Religious Service."

Since the time of Lewin and his collaborators, the objectives of the groups have changed considerably. No longer do most of them train leaders to deal with group tensions, to use the knowledge of group psychology to solve problems. The goals now are to have the group members reach their highest potentials, to improve them in every possible way, to banish all psychic tension and conflict, to turn on to nature and to people. It is more than group dynamics, or group psychotherapy, or the group relations of Bion have ever promised.

3 Toward Greater Awareness

The goals and methods of the sensitivity phenomenon are not determined always by scientific investigations and findings. The methods of the traditional T-groups were developed from research studies of how small groups function. Its aims have been to use the group processes constructively to train and educate people. These groups later moved from training-education and problem-solving to changing individuals. This, in moderation, has also been utilization of the forces inherent in the group, because emotional involvement, as well as the intellectual participation of the members, is a part of the group interaction. These groups are not committed to any particular philosophy or ideology extraneous to the group processes, nor do they depend on a leadership which is at its roots authoritarian.

The objectives of other groups is a personal growth which is variously defined depending on the scientific and philosophical viewpoints of the leaders. These groups tend to be organized around leaders whose forceful styles attract a devoted following. They do not allow the processes of the group to determine the outcome of the group interactions, but manipulate the group members to achieve the results they feel are desirable.

Marathon encounters, nude or with clothes, sometimes played back to the participants on videotape, are the most spectacular of these encounters. Gestalt therapy, Rolfing, bio-energetics, are others. Esalen is one of the growth centers where one can experience and examine all of these methods and many more. There are perhaps hundreds of these centers, but the most elaborate is Esalen. There are also centers which consist of no more than a suburban living room and a leader who has been to one or more encounters and who desires to pass on his new and wonderful knowledge to his friends and neighbors.

What are their goals? Growth, achievement of human potential, awareness, intimacy—all are very broad concepts and can include almost anything a person wishes them to include. Being able to communicate is growth; being able to make mature and enduring friendships and love relationships is growth; getting rid of prejudices is growth. Solving intrapsychic conflict, overcoming blocks to learning, overcoming sexual inhibitions which result in impotence, frigidity and other sexual problems, all lead to growth. No one could disagree. These objectives of the movement are desirable and reasonable. Do the sensitivity and encounter people always have desirable and reasonable goals in mind when they speak of growth and the achievement of optimum human potential? Does "growth" mean experiencing states of perceptual confusion and excitement to the point where they are called ecstasy? Is growth being able to tell a complete stranger that you have hostile feelings about him?

Treatment is often their goal, for normal persons, even for emotionally ill persons. Some claim their methods will cure physical illnesses. Dr. Perls said that myopia was often caused by tension; Alexander Lowen and Ida Rolf claim their methods of bodily relaxation will rid a person of many distressing physical symptoms.

If a person's viewpoint is not scientific, it is likely that his methods will not be scientific. I have already mentioned that the methods of the sensitivity training and encounter movement add up to an amazing assortment, from those which can bear the name of skillful techniques to those which should rightfully be called gimmicks. There are spirited debates among the faithful whether a particular method is authentic or artificial. This debate is usually decided by declaring it is right if it feels right, feeling right being the standard which all must accept. Dr. Elizabeth Mintz, who leads marathon encounters, writes that using physical contact in these encounters is offering an artificial substitute for the real emotional contact, but she goes on to note "spontaneous" physical contact frequently occurs in her marathons.[1]

Examples of nonverbal exercises are the "blind walk" and "eye-balling." These are often used as warm-up exercises, to accelerate the getting acquainted process in a new group, to accustom participants to use their senses in a new way. In one form of the "eye-balling" exercise, the participants hold hands in two parallel lines and make eye contact for about thirty seconds with the person opposite them. They move on to the next person in line, repeating the exercise. The idea is that if the usual verbal exchanges which block perception are eliminated, people will see one another more realistically. In the "blind walk," one participant is blindfolded and is led by another around the immediate physical environment and is exposed to a variety of sensory experiences, so that he makes use of all of his senses except sight to experience the environment. These are useful to a degree; they are hardly threatening to most persons. There are other nonverbal and contact methods which can arouse a considerable anxiety. One of these is known as the "Press," a way of expressing aggression. If two members of a group are struggling verbally with each other, they act out this struggle. One puts his hands on the other's shoulders, and against his resistance, forces him to the ground. Then the positions are reversed and the one who has been the victim becomes the aggressor.

The leader of the NTL groups undergo a special training program and on successfully completing this training are familiar with a battery of tested methods. Some of these leaders have come from backgrounds of scientific training and have worked in mental health fields. Others have no training or connection with these professions, but come from religion, the humanities, the arts. Some have had no training or experience in any type of helping or other profession. But they all receive training in the use of group methods.

From the same sources come the leaders of the other types of sensitivity training and encounter groups. The difference is that there are no training requirements for these leaders. Some have had professional training and use this training in a responsible way, but others who have had scientific training use methods which can hardly be called scientific, and indeed contradict some important areas of medical and psychological knowledge. A number of writers see no need for training and are not alarmed at the idea of disturbed persons being in encounter groups whose leaders have had no experience with handling emotionally ill persons, and indeed often deny the existence of emotional illness. One writer said:

> It is quite evident that many recent studies of the efficacy of treatment lead to the simple conclusion that the relatively untrained person does as well and sometimes better than we who have knocked around in academic halls and training institutes for some of the best years of our lives.[2]

Ideas such as this are used as justification for the lack of training of leaders, when they should be taken as indications that we might take a closer look at how we can better select and train people.

The leaders and followers of the sensitivity phenomenon take many ideas which have a core of truth and meaning and carry these ideas to extremes, or misapply them to the situations of the persons in their groups. This is the characteristic way of the cultist and of the fanatic, who simplify reality by ignoring things that limit or contradict their beliefs. It is also characteristic of the cultist or the fanatic to believe he has a new understanding, has gained a new awareness that no one before him has had.

One of the philosophies which leaders of the sensitivity movement have adopted is that of humanism. This is fundamentally an ethical system which emphasizes the dignity and worth of each human. It deals with the complex ethical problems of conscience, freedom and authority without reference to the existence of a supernatural life or a supernatural Being. Apart from this definition, there is no unified view among humanists. Some are conservative and hold to the eighteenth-century ideas of human progress which were expressed in the Enlightenment. This group includes many who are active in the sensitivity training and encounter movement. They differ from the earlier humanists only in that they have put feeling in place of reason as the means by which the improvement of the human race will come about. There are others in the humanist group who disagree with earlier propositions about the inevitability of man's progress.

The humanist opposes constraint and control of the individual and sees modern technological Western civilization as the chief instrument of this oppressive control. Humanism today is allied to the themes of existentialism, the themes of personal freedom, the assertion of selfhood, the yearning to rescue man from dehumanization. There is in existentialism the tendency to place importance on the experiencing of the present. Humanism echoes the belief of the Enlightenment, "the belief that all human beings can attain here on this earth a state of perfection hitherto in the West thought to be possible only for Christians in the state of grace, for them only after death."[3] Dr. Erich Fromm is one of the humanists in psychology whose writings are highly regarded by those in the sensitivity movement. He describes humanism as "the belief in the unity of the human race and man's potential to perfect himself by his own efforts."[4]

Humanism rejects authoritarian control in religion, in education, in child-rearing, in politics and in industry. Some feel the educators and the psychiatrists and the psychologists repress mankind and they urge their control be rejected as in times past when they urged the rejection of control by the theologians and the clergy. The humanists see a cleavage between the science-based culture and the humanities-based culture. A psychologist with a humanistic philosophy may reject diagnosis and psychological testing on the grounds that they classify and label people and so dehumanize them. He may not subject his methods and ideas to scientific research because he is convinced this research treats persons as things. When the research concerns relationships, especially the treatment relationship, it is injurious, in his view, because it interferes with the genuineness and spontaneity of the relationship.

This humanistic outlook at times degenerates into anarchy. Since the beginning of modern technology, there has been opposition to its methods and to the changes it brought about in peoples' lives. In the beginning of the nineteenth century, the Luddites, textile workers of England, smashed the machines in the factories to protest the takeover of the machine. Henry Thoreau wrote that we had become the tool of our tools. Max Stirnir advocated complete individualism, the assertion of one's self at the expense of state and family. This was the supreme goal, and to reach it, any action, including rebellion, was justified. There are humanists who are serious scholars and men of vision and there are those who espouse the philosophy of humanism but are really anarchists or disturbed persons who distort the reasonable basis of humanism. The writings of revolutionaries like Che Guevara and Franz Fanon appeal to them.

The humanist movement in present-day psychology has been named the 'Third Force," seeing itself as an alternative to both psychoanalysis and behaviorism which have been the dominant forces in psychology. The humanistic psychologists are of the opinion that psychoanalysts and behaviorists manipulate and exploit people. They alter the person's mind by means of insight and conditioning.

Closely related to the humanistic movement in psychology, if not actually a part of it, is the "Human Potential Movement—" the same persons who have been identified with humanistic psychology. Among them, Abraham Maslow, Carl Rogers and Herbert Otto have been in the forefront of the Human Potential Movement.

The notion that everyone has untapped resources that he could use if only he were given the opportunity, or if he were properly motivated, is not new. Advertisments in magazines tell people how they can become professional writers or artists, how they can become effective public speakers, guitar players or fashion models. At the turn of the century the psychologist, Henry James, wrote that a person uses only ten percent of his potential abilities. In the 1930s, a book, **Wake Up and Live** carried the inspirational message that we can all be better than we are. The book was a best seller.

Those prominent in the Human Potential Movement declare that we have not yet discovered the full range of human potential, that everyone is in some way gifted. If a person seems to be lacking in ability or believes he is inferior to others, this appearance and belief is due to lack of opportunity or is due to emotional causes. The emotional causes can be removed, the environment can be changed, to provide the needed opportunity so that everyone can develop his potential. The literature of the Human Potential Movement gives examples of extraordinary physical feats and mental accomplishments which have come about under conditions of unusual stress or after rigorous training. Dr. Otto approvingly quotes a Vasili Dovydov of the Moscow Institute of Psychology who wrote: "If we were able to force our brain to work at only half its capacity, we could, without any difficulty whatever, learn forty languages, memorize the large Soviet Encyclopedia from cover to cover, and complete the required courses in dozens of colleges."[5]

These ideas apply not just to education, but to all fields of human endeavor. Mental hygiene fits into this scheme. The psychologists and psychiatrists have been too occupied with the pathology of mental life, they say, and do not pay enough attention to the healthy parts of a person. If they did, they would be kept busy providing people with opportunities to reach their potential instead of trying to patch up ill people. Mental hygiene is attaining one's potential. A person who uses his potential is not just a healthy person; he has attained a state of "high level wellness."[6]

If one accepts this position, there is no limit to what people can do. One is limited only by the limitations of one's fantasies. Assertions are made in the name of reaching new heights of personal fulfillment; goals are put before people which are beyond the reach even of exceptional persons. The Human Potential Movement people take their statements seriously, and hold out to everyone the promise of great things. They promise as much, even more, than many religious and political leaders promise, and one of the means to attain these ends is sensitivity training and encounter.

To take an example of these promises: The writings of the sensitivity movement and of the Human Potential Movement frequently mention transcendental experiences. People should strive to have these experiences and everyone is capable of having them.

What are these important transcendental experiences?

The transcendent is beyond the boundaries of human experience, and it appears this is generally what these writers mean by the term. Beyond this, there seems to be little agreement on what a transcendental experience is. Some describe it as a "deep, genuine caring for others," or a "real feeling of harmony." As others use the term, it refers to the occurrence of a crisis, a state of excitement and adventure; it is being "turned on all the way." Others see in it a religious quality and seek ecstatic states, and states of mystical union, bliss, and identification with God. Some persons do not consider psychotic episodes to be abnormal mental conditions, but transcendental experiences.

Related to the transcendental experiences are the "peak experiences" of which Abraham Maslow writes. The peak experiences "is a generalization for the best moments of the human being, for the happiest moments of life, for experiences of ecstasy, rapture, bliss, of the greatest joy."[7] Both the transcendental and the peak experiences can refer to phenomena which are beyond the normal, and more specifically religious and mystical phenomena. The peak experience is the ultimate in turning on, and it can occur when a person has reached a high state of self-awareness. All means of consciousness-expanding techniques can be used: psychedelic drugs, hypnotism, sensory-awakening exercises, meditation, confrontations. In his book, **The Explorations in Human Potentialities,** Herbert Otto has a chapter written by Charlotte Selver on sensory awareness, and by Frederick Perls on gestalt therapy. This illustrates my position that there is no scientific rigor in elaborating hypotheses or in defining terms and concepts. Just about everything is acceptable.

Therapists and leaders of groups have become entranced with some of Maslow's ideas and have attempted to apply them in their work. Allied to the ideas of reaching one's fullest potential is Maslow's concept of "self-actualization." This, according to Maslow, "means experiencing fully, vividly, selflessly, with full concentration and total absorption. . . . At this moment of experiencing, the person is wholly and fully human. This is a self-actualizing moment."[8] He says also that it is " . . . experiencing without self-awareness, of making the growth choice rather than the fear choice, of listening to the impulse voices, of being honest and taking responsibility."[9]

Maslow's concepts are not new. He has given a new name to a state which others have attempted to describe. Psychologists and psychoanalysts have written about an "instinct to master" (Ives Hendricks), "self-realization" (Karen Horney), "Affectance Motivation" (Robert White), "Self-determinance" (Chris Argyris), "The Pro-active Personality" (Hubert Bonner). Whether there is such a striving to transcend the usual limitations of a person's actual existence, some inner drive to perfect one's self, is open to question. Whether the activity described comes from normal developmental processes, or is a neurotic striving, is another question.

Maslow's peak experiences are considered by many as goals of the processes of gaining more self-awareness and more awareness of reality. Encountering procedures and all the other procedures I have listed are roads to these experiences. Maslow writes that the peak experiences are "transient moments of self-actualization. . . . They are moments of ecstasy which cannot be bought, cannot be guaranteed, cannot even be sought. . . . Practically everyone does have peak experiences, but not everyone knows it."[10] Maslow also referred to the peak experience in religious terms, calling it a revelation "of the sacred."

While some in the sensitivity movement are of the opinion that everyone can have these marvelous experiences and can actualize his vast potential, Maslow feels only a few people can actualize themselves. Yet he does hold out to everyone this hope when he says that practically everyone has peak experiences. It is not difficult to account for the appeal of these ideas. They beckon a person to join an elite group, a specially favored company of those who can rise above the limits of the usual monotonous existence, who experience a greater awareness than others, a more majestic sense of self, and extraordinary, ineffable states of ecstasy. They are beautiful people.

The group experience is considered especially valuable in helping a person to reach his potential and actualize himself. In the group, the person is exposed to a provocative, stimulating, challenging, exciting environment, and he is enabled to overcome his inhibitions and his excessive control of his feelings and thoughts to such a degree that he is able to become a whole person. In the group he takes risks; he cannot withdraw. He must remove his masks, take off his armor, and honestly reveal himself. In this way he can reach his potential. Many feel the only way a person can reach his potential is through these evocative means, and this explains their strong commitment to changing the educational system. Carl Rogers said that what can be taught to a person is of no consequence, only that which is brought out from within him is significant.[11] This is another of the sayings and slogans the people in the sensitivity training and encounter movement are fond of. Catchy, appealing and profound observations of the human condition they seem to be. Mostly they are oversimplifications of very complex situations. Some take this statement of Rogers to mean that education should be only experiencing, turning on, without structure or discipline. They cite the offbeat ideas which A. S. Neill put into practice at his school, Summerhill, as the educational programs which will bring about this real learning. They forget, or may not even have been aware, that the children described in Neill's book, **Summerhill**, were certainly emotionally disturbed children.

Many persons are unfulfilled, are crippled, by neurotic conflicts and are denied the necessary opportunities for normal emotional growth. There is no question about these facts; there is nothing new or startling about this. The Human Potential Movement in moderation is a necessary reminder to all of us who need to be motivated. These movements are cruel, however, when they promise what they cannot deliver, when they stir up hopes which they cannot satisfy in lonely, unhappy people. Not only are they cruel, but they could be dangerous. A fanatic, a demagogue might find in the excesses of these movements a ready-made vehicle for his cause. In many ways, the sensitivity phenomenon has the appearance of a crusade, and the humanistic and human potentials concepts can give an element of respectability to the movement. After all, it is difficult to oppose the goal of the betterment of the human race.

When psychoanalysis states that suffering cannot be eliminated entirely—and indeed suffering, toleration of frustration and anxiety are necessary for growth—it is criticized by those in the sensitivity movement. Herbert Marcuse writes of a society "in which the abolition of poverty and toil terminates in a universe where the sensuous, the playful, the calm, the beautiful become forms of existence. . . . and thereby the form of society itself." Theodore Roszak writes that

> the primary object of our counter culture: (is) to proclaim a
> new heaven and earth so vast, so marvelous that the inor-
> dinate claims of technical expertise must of necessity with-
> draw in the presence of such splendor to a subordinate and
> marginal status in the lives of men. . . . We must be prepared
> to entertain the astonishing claim that men like Blake lay
> before us: that there are eyes which see the world not as com-
> monplace sight or scientific scrutiny sees it, but see it trans-
> formed, made lustrous beyond measure.[12]

In situations of extreme stress, some individuals have been
able to accomplish extraordinary things. There are persons who
have survived concentration camps, persons who have kept
their sanity under conditions of extreme sensory deprivation.
Athletes, scholars and religious devotees can at times surpass
themselves. Many of these are responses to an emergency, and
the "vast untapped resources" of the individual, which all sup-
posedly possess, are largely emergency resources, not suitable
for daily living. Persons whose fires burned constantly at this
intensity would soon be depleted. The major questions about
some of the sensitivity training programs concern this matter.
How effective are these programs for daily living? How long
can a person keep being turned on? How much stress can a person be subjected to without breaking down?

It is also true that some of the persons who have accomplished supra-normal things have done so because they were
not healthy. Examples are the paranoid, the religious and
political fanatic, the severely obsessive-compulsive person.
Others who go through these experiences often pay a heavy
price in terms of personality damage. Many of those who survived the concentration camps suffered lifelong hurts; they were
unable to integrate their experience into normal living.

Some may use real or supposed biological and social
limitations as reasons for not trying, but this does not mean that

there are no biological or social determinants of a person's potentials. Yet, in the human potential movement, there are some who take this position. If we examine this closely, we find a lack of agreement, as we find in many other areas of the sensitivity training and encounter movement. There are some who are convinced that there are social and developmental influences which are decisive for human growth and that lack of these can limit a person's potential, and that nurture is a determinant of human behavior and human aspirations. These persons do not rely entirely on the encountering but advocate programs beginning in early infancy, programs to insure that a person's optimum potential will be developed. For example, Veroff, reviewing the literature on motivation, writes that among the experiences necessary for a person as an adult to have a high achievement interest is the relationship of this person when he was an infant with a mother who had a "nurturant" attitude toward him. It is also necessary that his parents provide him with the correct amount of "moderately strong but consistent pressure for the achievement of mastery."

Norman O. Brown, with his proposal to foster in persons a "Dionysian Ego" in order to expand consciousness, belongs somewhere in the list of those who seek to reach these heights of human potential. So do Carl Jung, Viktor Frankl, Erich Fromm and Carl Rogers. Each sees man's capacities as unlimited. Here also belongs the Jesuit paleontologist, Teilhard de Chardin, who wrote of the convergence of the human race towards an "Omega Point," a final state of superconsciousness.

I do not mention these to give the impression that they are all identified with the movement, but to show that the ideas of the advertisers of sensitivity training and encounter are not original. One of the early sources of these ideas was the psychoanalyst, Otto Rank, who published his major works in the 1920s. Rank left the fold of orthodox psychoanalysis because of many things, one of them being his advocacy of "Will Training." Rank's aim was that the patient come to accept himself because he was accepted by other persons. In Rank's scheme, the therapist let the patient be aware that he accepted him, and in the formulation of sensitivity training and encounter, it is the group who accepts the person, confers on him self-acceptance and assures him that he can attain the fulfillment of his potential, can have peak experiences.

Drugs—mind-altering, consciousness-expanding, psychedelic drugs—are related to the sensitivity phenomenon. It had long been known that mescaline, psilocybin and opium could alter perceptions and feelings. In the early 1950s, two drugs, later known as tranquilizers, were introduced into the treatment of the mentally ill, and they revolutionized the care of these patients. It was the first large-scale use in this country of drugs which had a pronounced effect on mental functions. What the connection of these drugs was with the wider use of other mind-altering drugs by persons outside the scientific community, I do not know. LSD has been used by researchers to study its effects on disturbed patients, but until this time it has not produced significant results. In the early 1960s some psychologists, theologians and other "introspective" adults began to use mescaline, psilocybin, and particularly LSD in order to study their mind-altering effects. Aldous Huxley in the 1950s had taken mescaline and described his experience of ecstasy in his book, **The Doors of Perception**; he was later joined by others in the search for chemical ecstasy.

One of the connections of the use of psychedelic drugs with the sensitivity training and encounter movement is this: many who have become prominent in the movement had earlier tried drugs and then found they could produce the same effects with encounter methods. Bernard Gunther, who developed the sensory awakening techniques, took LSD before he developed these methods. Rasa Gustaitis in her book on the movement quotes him:

. . . Suddenly a new world of possibilities opened up to me. I had shut myself off in muscular tightness. I felt a physical deadness and also a deadness of sensitivity and emotions.

With LSD I realized that life was synonymous with flow and openness, feelings and sensation.[13]

Others in the sensitivity training movement have used psychedelic drugs, including Schutz and Perls. In the early 1960s, when Perls worked as a psychiatrist at the Mendecino State Hospital in California, he took LSD several times. He told Rasa Gustaitis that at first it made him "really paranoic," but he continued to take it because it was "something that made life worth experiencing." When he took psilocybin he said that he re-experienced a "life and death struggle" he had undergone after he had had a stroke.

It was the position of these and others that when a person used these drugs he could see himself in a more honest way; he could see the artifical aspects of his life. The drug jolted him out of his "mind-set," out of his customary way of looking at himself and the world. He was more open to experience, more sensitive to people. LSD brought him face-to-face with the mysteries of life and of the universe. It allowed him to have a transcendent and a mystical experience and it gave him the answers to the questions of identity and the meaning of life. He could become fused with the ultimate reality.

Walter Houston Clark, a former professor of the Psychology of Religion at Andover Newton Theological Center, Massachusetts, has written of the alleged relationships between these drugs, religious experiences and mental health. He appears to accept at face value the assertions of persons like Dr. Timothy Leary, Dr. Humphry Osmond and Aldous Huxley that the altered states of consciousness and perception resulting from LSD and other drugs are indeed religious states. He also feels that empathy is a result of psychedelic experiences because the person who is under the influence of these drugs feels at one with others.

. . . empathy often does result from psychedelic experiences. It grows naturally out of the experience of unity. If one identifies himself with all things, it follows that he feels at one with his fellow creatures and so acknowledges responsibility towards them.[14]

The psychedelic drug experience has appealed to many persons with a humanistic outlook on life, with a commitment to expanding human potential, because they have felt it made them aware of the split between men and nature. It also made many of these persons more receptive to those philosophies of the East which seek a unity of man with nature. Huxley, Leary and Alan Watts have described the psychedelic drug experience in terms of Eastern mysticism. Dr. Richard Alpert, a psychologist who was associated with Leary in the Harvard drug experiments, eventually became Rama Bass Dam and settled in California as a Buddhist teacher. He has also given seminars at Esalen.

The meandering roads of the sensitivity movement lead to many destinations, and one of these is religion. The sensitivity training and encounter persons are not at all rigid or sectarian or prejudiced when it comes to the matter of religion. Whatever a person wishes to call religion seems acceptable; it can be a completely private and personal religion without dogma, clergy or church. There can be a variety of religious leaders, holy men of Eastern religions, charismatic group leaders. It is also quite acceptable to work within the organized churches.

To live more fully, to experience more deeply, to find the answers to existence are the questions religion attempts to answer, although some religions say that not all of the answers can be found in this life. A number of religious persons have been attracted to the sensitivity training and encounter movement, especially in the Episcopalian and Roman Catholic churches. In the early 1960s, before the flourishing of sensitivity training and encounter groups, the Roman Catholic Church underwent many changes. These involved many of the external forms of worship, modifying the elaborate and outdated ceremonies, using the vernacular in place of Latin, bringing the church up to date. Although many of these changes were superficial, they were important to many persons. They took from many of the faithful the props with which religion had supported their beliefs, and these persons joined the numbers of alienated persons who sought answers in sensitivity training and encounter. The "death of God" movement in theology was flourishing, and religious persons were exhorted to turn their interest to the world which until then they had been taught to consider alien and dangerous. Theologian Harvey Cox became known for his work, **The Secular City**, which showed religion and salvation in the things of the world. Professor Cox went on to become active in the programs of Esalen.

The death of God movement seems to have died a few years ago, to be replaced by the theology of hope, and the theologians were of the opinion that the secular type of religion was not enough. They saw a need to go beyond the secular, to return to ritual, emotion and mysticism. Outside the church, persons found their mystical turn-ons through drugs, meditation, witchcraft and a multitude of other things, including sensitivity training and encounter. In the church there was a revival of pentecostalism, and also a rush to sensitivity training and encounter. Cox was able to shift with the times and wrote of the need to have inner religious experiences and for a theology of celebration.

There is yet another way to seek the three goals I have listed: to live more fully, to experience more deeply, to find the answers to existence. It is to seek them in pleasure. Dr. Alexander Lowen, one of the leaders in the "Body Biz" part of the sensitivity movement, and who has influenced Schutz, entitled one of his books **Pleasure**. Titillative, erotic, orgastic pleasure is available today in ways it was not so readily available in former times. It is admitted by some of the adherents of encounter, as well as by some of its critics, that many go to encounters in order to obtain sensory experiences. It appears that the writings of some in the movement are directed more, and often almost exclusively, toward means of attaining sensual pleasures.

Bernard Gunther wrote an article for a recent issue of *Playboy*, complete with photographs. The sensory awakening he was describing and illustrating did not seem different from some types of sexual foreplay. Dr. Arthur Burton, who writes about encounters and also leads them, wrote this:

> . . . . Many clients tell me they go to encounter group centers not only for the encounter itself but for the vast opportunities for sexual experience which are to be found there. One famous encounter center offers baths in which mixed nude bathing is the rule after the sessions themselves. One invariably gets a chance there to live sexuality rather than learning how to displace or sublimate it.[15]

The contention is that we are free now because we are uninhibited sexually. At the same time that there has been the enormous growth of the sensitivity phenomenon, the laws have been changed to remove restrictions concerning sex in books, movies and other forms of entertainment. Nudity, as well as varieties of heterosexual and homosexual experiences, if not more prevalent, are at least more widely publicized.

The byword of the sensitivity movement—Do it in the here-and-now—is related to this pursuit of pleasure. Here-and-now can mean no frustration, no postponement of gratification; and this is an important part of the sensual way of life. Critics of this are called repressive and puritanical. One of those critics was Freud. Freud did feel that civilization often was too repressive, but he recognized that human nature is so fashioned that man must struggle to control his impulses, not to seek endless sensual experiencing.

4 | The Leaders and Their Methods

All of these elements of the sensitivity phenomenon, its humanistic philosophy, its endeavor to expand awareness and to activate potential, its search for religious experience and for bodily pleasure, are at the Esalen Institute. Almost all of the persons of prominence in the movement have been at Esalen. Most of the encounter techniques have been tried there; many of them have originated there. It is the most widely publicized of the growth centers, has given rise to numerous offspring, and attracts the largest number of persons to its sessions. It has, in the description of one writer, "the features of a hip spa, a mental clinic and a religious center."[1]

Esalen came into being soon after Michael Murphy, a man who had spent time studying Eastern religions, inherited a once fashionable and scenic spa with mineral baths at Big Sur, California. He invited a number of persons whose ideas he was interested in to give a series of weekend seminars at the spa. Among the first guest leaders were Alan Watts, an authority on Zen Buddhism, Dr. Paul Tillich, the noted existentialist theologian, Charlotte Selver, whose specialty was sensory awareness, and Dr. Abraham Maslow, a prominent psychologist who was one of the leaders of the humanistic movement in psychology. The first seminars were given in 1962, and Esalen had become in a few years a year-round center offering a variety of encounter groups to several thousand persons each year. In addition to conducting encounter groups, it now publishes books and tapes, trains encounter group leaders, works with community agencies, educational systems and church groups. Above all else, its staff strives diligently to make Esalen widely known.

One way to describe the extreme sensitivity training and encounter groups is to say that they have carried every idea just about as far as it can go. They have used these ideas and methods without relating them to other relevant findings. Getting to see ourselves as others see us, being able to question our beliefs, being able to tell ourselves and others what we really feel and think, being able to love others and to accept the loving offered by others—all are worthwhile goals of individual and group treatment. However, the leaders of the movement tend to see all of this as suitable in the fullest measure for all persons at all times. Sensitivity training and encounter have taken on many features of the counter-culture of the 1960s and adopted the ideas of many of its propagandists, as well as some of the styles of living and dressing of its devotees. Paul Goodman, one of the thinkers of the counter-culture, joined with Dr. Frederick Perls and Ralph Hefferline to write the book **Gestalt Therapy,** one of the sources for encounter group methods.

Harvey Cox, a Baptist theologian who taught at Harvard and became a leader in the theological changes, and Sam Keen, another theologian, who proposed a "Dionysian" religious view, founded on sensuality and impulse gratification, joined the staff at Esalen. Professor Joseph Campbell, a scholar steeped in the religions of the East, had taught for many years at Sarah Lawrence College. Professor Campbell lectured at Esalen and his book, **The Hero With a Thousand Faces,** which had been first published in 1949, became a best seller. Those who could not find the answers they sought in Western philosophy and religion turned to Watts and Campbell and others at Esalen to learn the wisdom of the East. So did those who were looking for a new high. George Leonard, an educator; the anthropologists Joseph Henderson, Claudio Naranjo and Houston Smith; the psychiatrists John Lilly, Joel Fort, Stanislav Grof; as well as Rollo May, Buckminster Fuller, Viktor Frankl, Ronald Laing and Aldous Huxley are among those listed on Esalen's roster.

There are several leaders we can take a closer look at, for they are the most prominent in the movement at Esalen and at other centers.

There is Dr. William Schutz, psychologist, associate at Esalen, author of several books describing the techniques he and others use. Schutz is not important for his ideas, for he shows little originality and borrows freely from many sources. He accepts Reichian ideas, yoga, predestination, reincarnation, the massage which is called rolfing, muscle relaxation therapy, nonverbal communication and many other ideas and methods. Nor is he important for his gifts as a therapist, nor because he is a thorough and objective scientist. He is none of these. He is important because this part of the sensitivity phenomenon is a cult and he is one of its most zealous and effective evangelists; it is a product to be sold and he is a vigorous salesman. He is typical of many individuals prominent in some forms of sensitivity training and encounter: aggressive, exhibitionistic, so enamored of his gimmicks that he is unable to have any perspective on them. He is one of the leaders whom Jane Howard called the "circuit riders."

. . . In the spiritual life of this century they occupy a niche similar to that of the itinerant preachers in the last. They travel by jet instead of horseback, covering a nation instead of a county, but the message is not much different. The kingdom of heaven, they say in their various jargons, is within: within you and me and within us all. . . . By whatever name they are called, the circuit riders make their rounds with great style, at times resembling alchemists and tribal witch doctors. Behavior science not withstanding, their rituals seem mysterious and primitive. They are engaged, sometimes quite literally, in the laying on of hands and the exorcism of devils. Their heady mission is to open people, to free them from their inhibitions and help them to rise up to and beyond their limits. . . . Circuit riders must indeed have unabrasive voices, showmanship, finesse and infinite tact. . . . The styles of trainers and leaders are as distinctive as those of mezzo-sopranos, abstract painters or skiers. Some are so restrained as to seem almost stuffy. . . . But some prefer top-volume noise, primary colors, and maximum risk. Of these the most conspicuous is Schutz.[2]

Schutz earned a Ph.D. in psychology at the University of California at Berkeley, taught several years at universities in the East, including Harvard and Brandeis, where Maslow was professor of psychology, and trained in T-group methods at Bethel, Maine. He wrote a few of the early papers on T-group methods. Like many of those who have been prominent in the West Coast movement, he had used the hallucinogenic drugs and he believes that these drug trips are a "valuable experience." He had also tried psychoanalysis, but felt that it had not helped him. *

Schutz became associated with Esalen, put his ideas and methods into a book called **Joy** and another called **Here Comes Everybody.** Both books are filled with ideas from the counterculture, with long-discredited ideas from the fringe of the medical and psychiatric professions. He attempts to fuse these into a method of treatment and training, and the results of this attempt are, in the words of one reviewer, "prodigies of oversimplification."[4]

Dr. Frederick S. Perls, who was working at Esalen at the time of his death in 1970, was one of the hallowed figures there.

---

* Jane Howard reports Schutz saying: "The reason people stay in analysis for eight or nine years is that they never have to confront anything. Nobody ever pushes them. I experienced this in my own 600-hour analysis. I was so clever I just didn't get much out of it."[3]

Called "Fritz" by those in the movement, Dr. Perls was a psychiatrist and a psychoanalyst who received his training in Berlin, first with the psychoanalyst Karen Horney in 1925, with several other psychoanalysts, and finally, with the analyst, Wilhelm Reich. In the early years of his professional life, he considered himself part of the mainstream of psychoanalysis and read a paper at the famous Marienbad Psychoanalytic Congress in 1936. In later years he abandoned the practice of psychoanalysis. He came to the United States in 1947, and with the help of Dr. Erich Fromm and Dr. Clara Thompson, who were prominent dissenters from classical psychoanalysis, he became established in New York City. There he worked for a time with Charlotte Selver, of sensory-awakening fame. After wandering about the United States and other countries, having psychedelic trips on LSD and psilocybin, he finally settled at Esalen. It is of interest that in his earliest years, before he studied medicine, this flamboyant figure studied drama at the Max Reinhardt Theatre in Berlin.

Rasa Gustaitis, in her book, **Turning On,** called Perls a "guru" and wrote that he was "much more like a Zen master than the standard American psychotherapist." She said also that he was a "magician-impressario" and his seminars were "performances."[5]

In brief, Perls' gestalt therapy is this: When a person's *concept* of himself and of reality is distorted it is because his *perception* of himself and reality is distorted. The gestalt theory of Wertheimer, on which Perls appears to base his work, states that a whole is more than the sum of its parts and analyzing the parts does not provide information about the essence of the whole. Gestalt theory is a valid description of how people perceive, although not a complete explanation of psychic functions. The configuration, or gestalt, which a person perceives, depends not only on what is actually present to be perceived, but also depends on the needs of the person who perceives. In explaining this, Perls used the example of a man who wishes to mail a letter. Until he mails it, he is preoccupied with the idea of finding a mailbox and this configuration may interfere with his ability to focus on other things. Once he has mailed the letter, this need will not be in the center of his awareness.

Perls believed that people seek to escape from experiences or "awarenesses" which are unpleasant, and this produces a block in their emotional growth and in their ability to perceive the wholeness of reality. Gestalt therapy removes these blocks to full awareness. In the encounter, the person becomes aware of the block and an impasse results. The therapist's task is to force the patient through the impasse. Words like "exploding" are used to describe this procedure. When a person can overcome the impasse, he no longer has a neurotic symptom.

At his Esalen encounters, Perls sat at the head of the group and next to him was a red chair which he called (of course!) the "hot seat." A person with a problem sat in the hot seat. While the members of the group watched, or participated in a limited way as co-therapists, Perls engaged the person in the hot seat in a spirited, seductive, bullying confrontation. We should note that Bion has called to our attention that this is not a group procedure, but rather an individual procedure with an audience. In fact, Perls did not believe in group processes, and felt that change took place only in an I-Thou relationship. Perls encouraged and prodded the person to become completely open. Gustaitis wrote how he challenged the participants, yawned and slept when bored, exaggerated his responses, " . . . was often rude, arrogant, inconsiderate—sometimes outrageous" and he refused "to acknowledge any encounter other than one that is completely natural and direct."

By a variety of techniques, Perls attempted to locate the "missing" experience that he believed caused the block, and once it was discovered he forced the person to face it. Perls felt that when an individual faced this impasse there was a "layer of implosion," a "death layer" made up of the feelings of loneliness, boredom and lack of meaning to life. In this, Perls uses the formulations of R.D. Laing, the British psychiatrist, whose ideas I would presume Perls was familiar with, since Laing had been at Esalen and his books have been very popular with the sensitivity movement people.

When the person reached the "layer of implosion," only two feelings were available to him—self-pity and anger. He had to choose to *explode* into strong emotions of anger, love, grief or joy. This explosion released energies which had been bound up in the neurosis and freed the person for a fullness of experiencing and creating. The explosions were moments of sudden and intense insight with heightened awareness of the present. Need I add that these assertions of Perls are not accepted by scientists? They are not verified, and I present them in some detail here only so that the reader can have some idea of the irrational ideas of Perls and others like him.

Rasa Gustaitis, writing of Esalen and referring especially to Perls' seminars, commented that " . . . the atmosphere here is charged with sexuality, intimacy, intensity. People come here to be jarred into some new aliveness, to have their minds turned around, and expect to see taboos crumble. Only phoney or affected behavior is unacceptable here. Madness, promiscuity, all forms of eccentricity are part of the scene."[6] Those who hope that the encounter movement is a shortcut to a new life (and most who go to encounters believe its magic will work instantly as all magic should), are bound to be disappointed, for Perls himself has said that each person must work through hundreds of impasses. It seems as if the encounters could last at least as long as Dr. Schutz' 600-hour analysis.

Dr. Carl R. Rogers is one of the prominent psychologists who have become a part of the sensitivity training and encounter movement. He coined the term "basic encounter group," and is director of the Center for the Study of the Person, in La Jolla, California. Rogers was well known before the beginnings of the sensitivity phenomenon and when he was teaching at the University of Chicago in the 1940s and 1950s he developed a system called "client-centered counseling." This treatment system made Dr. Rogers well known in the education and mental health professions.

I mention here some of the important characteristics of the client-centered counseling in order to contrast it with Roger's present views. In a much-quoted paper in 1957, he wrote that the essential attitudes which the counselor must have toward his client are empathy, unconditional positive regard and congruence (which he said is made up of genuineness and openness).[7] If the counselor has these qualities and the client perceives them, this is sufficient. Nothing else is needed for therapeutic change to occur. Psychoanalysts hold that change comes about through the resolution of intrapsychic conflicts or through alleviation of external stresses. Rogers held that this was not necessary. The goal in client-centered counseling is to have the client become intellectually aware of his problems, but not to *experience* them emotionally in the counseling relationship. The present, rather than the past, is emphasized, and the counselor must keep his own life and his own feelings out of the counseling relationship. Because the client perceives that the counselor has a positive regard for him, understands and accepts him, he has positive feelings for the counselor.

No one disputes that this positive regard, this rapport, is necessary in order that treatment may begin. It is not the entire treatment. It only brings about the conditions necessary for treatment.

Rogers abandoned many of the features of client-centered counseling when he became involved in encounters. Like others in the movement, he no longer considers rational thinking important. What is important and necessary is that the members of the group experience each other in an emotional way, that they encounter one another. Encounter, in fact, is defined in terms of expressing and perceiving the feelings of each in the group. Rogers defines basic encounter as coming into "much closer and more direct contact with one another than is customary in ordinary life." He gives the example from one of his encounters of a man telling of his feelings about the tragic death of his child, and one of the group responds: "I've never felt so close to another human being. I've never before felt a real physical hurt in me from the pain of another. I feel completely with you."[8] This, according to Rogers, is a basic encounter.

Rogers does not now hold that the counselor (he now calls him the facilitator) should keep his own feelings to himself and keep information about his personal life from the group. The facilitator uses the feelings which exist at the moment, and shares with the group his feelings about himself and about them. This self-revelation of the group leader is routine in the encounter group. In T-groups it is used sparingly; in the gestalt-therapy groups it is carried to an extreme. This can be harmful to the group, as Yalom and his associates showed in their study of encounter groups presented to the 1972 meeting of the American Psychiatric Association. At times this self-revelation of the leader is quite boring; Schutz' latest book is filled with this kind of self-revelation. It is not very interesting, useful or scientific.

Many therapists and group leaders feel as Rogers does, and they must express their feelings towards the members of their group in physical ways. One therapist writes: "I am now convinced that the therapist who will not touch a client with his body will not touch a client at all. . . . body participation is but another mode by which the therapist can communicate his deepest subjective self to the client."[9] It can be but a step from this to the "Love Treatment" advocated by psychiatrist Martin Sheppard.

Sensitivity training and encounter is not concerned just with a person's mind but also with his body. Bodily response and bodily awareness are important. Involvement of the body heightens one's awareness, expands one's consciousness and helps one to regress. Exercises are used as warm-ups in beginning groups, and as a means of breaking through resistances when the activity of the group comes to a standstill. Massage and muscular relaxation, breathing control and yoga are used to release the person from the bodily armor which encloses him. There are even more benefits. These exercises, and taking off one's clothes, will correct distortions of the body image and get rid of the hang-ups and inhibitions about the body. The perfect control of one's senses and bodily musculature leads to *satori* and to other mystical experiences.

One of the ancestors of this part of the sensitivity phenomenon is Dr. Wilhelm Reich, another of the early psychoanalysts who left the mainstream of the psychoanalytic movement. Reich's early works explained how a person's character structure was formed, and this was an important contribution. Reich described how a person wards off anxiety and controls his impulses by character traits, and how compulsive actions, phobic avoidances and other symptoms become part of his habitual behavior. These character traits free him from conscious anxiety, but restrict his personality growth, make him less flexible. In Reich's metaphor, which is regularly used by the sensitivity training and encounter people, the person is as rigid as if he were encased in a suit of armor. Reich called this the "armoring of character." To this extent, Reich's formulations are reasonable and acceptable. However, he went beyond reason, literally beyond reason, in his theories. In many places his writings show the mark of the psychosis which was more apparent in his later years.

Reich attempted to explain the armoring of character in bodily terms. He observed, as had many physicians before him, that a person's bodily states could change under the influence of emotions, and these changes persisted in certain persons. Obsessive-compulsive characters may have a rigid, unbending physical posture; hysterical characters are inclined to have rapid, shallow breathing and fainting spells. Like many of those who had come before him, Reich thought a disordered physiology was at fault, and the physical manifestation was the *cause* of the emotion. In his view the defenses are a muscular armor and the person's unconscious resistances are rooted in muscular rigidity. This explanation was sufficient for him, and he fashioned a treatment for character disturbances which he called "vegetotherapy." By this time, the early 1930s, Reich had left psychoanalysis. His vegetotherapy eventually was replaced by "orgone" therapy, and he claimed a "universal primordial energy" was the basis of all psychological activity. By a series of "experiments" which contradicted the most elementary data of biological chemistry and physics, Reich thought he had found the source of vital energy which was identical with sexual energy.

Perls had been analyzed by Reich. Indeed, some of Perls' ideas about energy sound very much like those of Reich. Perls' notions, as he expressed them in his book, **Ego, Hunger and Aggression,** show the same irrational thinking which characterizes most of Reich's later works. There is, for example, Perls' definition of anxiety as "excitement plus inadequate oxygen supply."[10]

Another follower of Reich is the psychiatrist, Alexander Lowen, who practices "bio-energetics." This stems from Dr. Lowen's peculiar ideas about human physiology and his unique interpretation of the mind-body relationship. His system contradicts the basic physiological facts which are taught not only to every medical student, but to every high school student who takes a course in human biology. It is this unscientific nonsense that Schutz and others in the movement take seriously.

Lowen writes that bio-energetic therapy is founded on the "functional identity" of body and mind. The closeness of his system to the delusional thinking of Reich is evident in passages such as this one:

. . . any real change in a person's thinking and, therefore, in his behavior and feeling, is conditioned upon a change in the functioning of his body. The two functions that are most important in this regard are *breathing* and *movement.* Both of these functions are disturbed in every person who has an emotional conflict by chronic muscular tensions that are released. . . .*Feeling* is determined by breathing and movement . . . Inadequate respiration produces anxiety, irritability, and tension. It underlies such symptoms as claustrophobia and agoraphobia. . . . the inability to breathe normally becomes the main obstacle to the recovery of emotional health.[11]

Lowen differentiates between schizoid individuals and neurotics on the basis that one inhibits his *inspiration* and the other his *expiration*. The remedy for all of these conditions is surprisingly simple: learn to breathe properly and to release muscular tension. Lowen gives elaborate breathing exercises and methods for releasing muscular tension. One passage in his writing is reminiscent of Reich's ideas about energy:

> The lumination of the human body is not just a metaphorical way of speaking. The human body is surrounded by a "force field" which has been described as an aura or an atmosphere. . . . This field or aura can be seen by the naked eye under certain conditions. It is shown in early Renaissance paintings as a glow about the heads of saints.[12]

This is like the doctrine of clairvoyance as described by the Theosophists. The clairvoyant is able to see the "causal body" of the undeveloped person as an "ovoid" surrounding his physical body.

> "As the ego develops, this bright matter of the causal body is stirred into alertness by vibrations which reach it from the lower bodies and it gradually becomes filled with matter of the most lovely and delicate hues."[13]

In 1918, Frederich Matthias Alexander wrote a fervent book he called **Man's Supreme Heritage.** He ascribed most of the ills of modern civilization to faulty breathing and he prescribed the conscious control of breathing as the way the human race could be regenerated. Perls refers to Alexander's "concentration" therapies several times in his writings.

In 1929 a physician named Edmund Jacobson wrote a book, **Progressive Relaxation,** which proposed the thesis that muscular tension produces the difficult breathing which often occurs in anxiety attacks. [15] Therefore, the constriction of the chest muscles *causes* anxiety. His treatment for anxiety was a program of exercises to relax these muscles. This method has been around for a long time and it would be little more than a historical curiosity had it not been enthusiastically and uncritically adopted by Lowen, Perls, Schutz and the whole array of gestalt therapists, sensory awareness devotees and allied groups.

Perls admitted his indebtedness to Jacobson, although he himself claimed to be more scientific. The inadequate supply of oxygen that Perls sees as one of the causes of anxiety comes from faulty breathing. A person overcomes his anxiety when he relaxes the constricting chest muscles and releases the bound-up excitement. To the breathing and muscular relaxation therapies of Lowen, Alexander and Jacobson, Perls added the concentration therapy of Alexander. He tells, for example, how to concentrate on the mastication of food. This, he believes, is important in handling one's aggression. Chewing each mouthful of food a prescribed number of times was proposed by a Dr. Fletcher some time ago as an aid to proper digestion, but now Perls has updated Fletcherism in the service of mental hygiene. The fact that Lowen, Jacobson and Perls are physicians does not, of course, guarantee that their ideas are medically or psychologically sound. But many are beguiled by these almost worthless therapies.

Massage is important in the encounters. It releases tension, promotes better circulation and increases sensory awareness. Both the sick and the healthy feel better. That it is pleasurable, relaxes tense muscles and results in a temporary feeling of well-being is true. That it cures illnesses and improves one's personality is not true. Of the many practitioners of massage in the movement, the most prominent are Charlotte Selver, Ida Rolf and Bernard Gunther. They have elaborated theories to explain how their brand of physical therapy works.

The persons I have written about are a few of the more prominent leaders in the extreme forms of the sensitivity training and encounter movement. The methods I have described, and the rationale for the methods, are only a few of the constantly growing collection of ideas and methods. There is no system, no unifying principles, nothing that can justify one calling the sensitivity phenomenon a scientific discipline or a rational treatment method.

Theories, Techniques
5 | and Treatment

Do sensitivity training and encounter groups give treatment? The first T-groups were not intended to treat but to train group leaders. They were designed to help the participants learn group dynamics and to apply their learning to the group problems in the "back home" settings of industry, politics and education.

In 1962, T-groups were called "group therapy for normals."[1] It was not long before the group procedures became treatment for everyone, normal or not. In a short time, the objectives of the sensitivity movement changed from training to treatment, although we must bear in mind that there are still T-groups that keep to the original purpose of training; there are also the highly structured groups of Dr. Bion, which are "work groups." As I noted in the first chapter, some groups say they do no treatment, although often they deny what is obviously happening. Or they say there is no difference between those who are called sick and those called healthy. Encounter is suitable for all. Others say they do treat disturbed persons and their treatments are superior to medical and psychiatric treatment.

If these group leaders are doing treatment, how do we judge this treatment? Is it indicated for the persons who are in these groups? Is it good or bad treatment?

Treatment of any kind is a service offered by a person who is professionally qualified, a service to persons who are in need of it and can be helped by it. I consider some forms of sensitivity training and encounter to be treatment and they should be evaluated as treatment. The training and goals and motivation of the leader, the relationship of the leader and his group members (the treatment relationship) and the methods of treatment all need to be evaluated.

Among the leaders of sensitivity training and encounter groups are well-trained professionals in the fields of psychiatry, psychology, social work and education, and who are competent to work with groups. There are also self-proclaimed trainers and facilitators who judge they are qualified to lead these groups because they have participated in sensitivity training or encounter groups. It is this last group of leaders who can do the most harm. Not only are they innocent of any knowledge of the psychic life of the individual and of the dynamics of groups, and hardly aware of the usefulness and limitations of the methods they use, but their own emotional condition may be disturbed and their motivation questionable. These comments about disturbed emotional states and questionable motivation can apply as well to some of the professionals connected with the movement.

Sensitivity training and encounter is *experiencing*. This can be a goal in itself so that some persons spend their free time, their weekends, looking for new ways of experiencing. This experiencing, they claim, can be a way to growth, emotional health, to religion. The literature abounds with glowing references to religion, to mystical experiences, to ecstasy. One of the psychologists at Esalen said that the meaning of Esalen was a "truly religious one."[2] This then, is a motivation of some leaders, to bring religion and ecstasy to the participants.

The leaders who have serious personality problems may not be able to keep these problems from influencing their work with groups. Some leaders are aggressive, even sadistic in their methods, and the group structure gives them the opportunity to release their aggression and to gratify their hostile impulses. Not only do they not see this as not harmful, but contend that it is good technique. Jane Howard quotes Dr. William Schutz as saying: "The further you go toward violence, sensuality and openness . . . the better trainer you are, almost linearly."[3] She further writes: " . . . Not one to shrink from novelty or extremes, Schutz asked men in one of his workshops to urinate in front of each other."[4] Bach, Perls, Bindrim, all employ a fiercely aggressive approach in their encounters. Dr. George Bach uses what he calls "constructive aggression" in his encounters. Synanon, the encounter program that began with drug addicts, has the doctrine that there must be "unrelenting attack" in groups. Carl Rogers, who expresses some warnings about an excess of aggression in groups, nonetheless believes that he must overtly relate to group members his hostile feelings about them. He writes that he said to one person in his group: "I woke up this morning feeling I never want to see you again."

I have noted the opinion that training is not necessary for an encounter group leader, that it is not even necessary for a therapist who treats mentally ill persons. This means that at best we have leaders who have good intentions, an ability to empathize with people, to say helpful things, and the good sense to know their limitations. Unfortunately, there are few of these "natural" leaders or therapists. Being gifted is not enough, and the same person who encourages untrained leaders to take on the great responsibility of working with the emotions of healthy or sick persons would not choose a poorly-trained surgeon if he needed an operation; would hardly choose a person who knew nothing about engines to repair his car's engine. Lack of training means that the therapist or leader does not have the means to recognize those signs and symptoms which indicate illness and he is unable to estimate the effect of his methods on the group members. It may also mean that he has no continuing sense of responsibility to the members of his group. This sense of responsibility is an attribute of most professionally trained persons; and, as all physicians know, treatment is also a legal responsibility. When the leader has no concern about the possibility of hurting people, when an individual or a group makes no effort to check on the outcome of its procedures, there is little responsibility, little of the caring and concern that the sensitivity training and encounter group people write about. Their disdain for research not only shows their anti-intellectual and anti-scientific bias, but also their lack of responsibility towards those they treat.

A trained person bases his treatment on the accurate diagnosis of a person's emotional condition. It is not enough to have a knowledge of the ways people in general develop and adapt. Generalizations about the needs of human beings, even when they are correct, are in themselves of limited help in understanding a particular person. It is misleading to assume that all a therapist needs to know are formula like the existential formula that man's source of anxiety is his fear of being alone. What is necessary to know is how *this individual* developed, how his constitution and his life history determine his feelings and thoughts and actions.

Most untrained leaders and some of the mental health professionals feel diagnosis is not necessary. Classification and diagnostic labels, they say, do not explain humanity and we should be interested in the "human-ness" of people, not in their differences. We should be interested in their healthy parts, not their sick parts. They justify this position by saying that we have been too concerned with pathology. There is no need to make distinctions between sick and well people because the same means are used to help both. Diagnosis is said to interfere with the relationship between patient and therapist, between group members and leader, to destroy spontaneity and creativity.

One psychologist, who has written on the marathon encounter groups and conducts these groups, views diagnosis as "irrelevant to marathon," yet the participants in her groups, *by her own diagnosis,* ranged from persons with borderline schizophrenia to persons who were clinically normal.[5] If it is assumed there is a common sickness, a malady which afflicts everyone, then there is no need of diagnosis. What works for one, works for all. It would save a great deal of time and effort and research if we could say the common sickness is alienation or dehumanization or lack of openness, and all everyone needs is love and openness. The reality is that each one of us becomes sick, just as each one of us will die, from an assortment of events and causes which affects each of us in a singular way, to which each responds as a unique human being. This is one reason for diagnosis, because each one has a special relation to his illness. No one can truly have the empathy which the sensitivity training and encounter people rightly say is so necessary, without recognizing and acting upon this truth. Another reason for diagnosis is that treatment or help cannot be prescribed without diagnosis. Finally, diagnosis is needed to keep from harming the patient.

A critic of the methods of the movement has written:

> . . . Screening procedures geared towards specific objectives can be of crucial importance. They are insufficiently employed and what are substituted in some instances are pious rationales, silent prayers that psychotic episodes will be avoided, and the hope that more people will benefit than not.[6]

Some leaders are not concerned about the members of their group suffering from emotional trauma and psychotic breakdowns. They do not conduct follow-up studies to determine if their procedures have harmed anyone. Some say that the encounter group is the ideal place to have a psychotic break because the support and closeness of the group will enable the person to reintegrate himself on a higher plane of functioning. Michael Murphy of Esalen is quoted in an interview which appeared in *Psychology Today*:

> It appears that the non-paranoid acute schizophrenic break is relatively short and is followed by a re-integrative process

so that the individual returns from his "trip" with a higher IQ than at the beginning.[7]

Nonsense! Worse that that, harmful nonsense. Murphy is not a professionally trained person and one could understand his not knowing much about schizophrenia. Unfortunately, professionals speak in the same way. Dr. Schutz, who is a clinical psychologist, described how a woman became psychotic during one of his encounters, and he argued that the experience was good for her.

These leaders and writers favor the views of the British psychiatrist, R.D. Laing, that persons become psychotic because of the pressures of society. The schizophrenic experience, Laing states, is therapeutic if it can be completed without interference by doctors, nurses, medicines or other treatments. Laing has established "blow-out centers" where schizophrenics can live in a communal arrangement without benefit of professional attention. They care for one another. *
Laing also believes a psychotic breakdown enables a person to liberate himself from his restricting defenses and to realize his potentials. This is his idea of a growth experience. It is a "trip," an "auto-initiatory voyage."

His viewpoints are not shared by most mental health professionals, who consider Laing's views irrational, without any validation. There is no evidence to support his belief that schizophrenia is a growth process. Biochemists, for example, have found that the bodily responses of schizophrenic patients often differ in many ways from other persons. Schizophrenia is one of the most serious of mental illnesses, an illness that fills more hospital beds in this country than all other sicknesses and injuries combined. Numerous hypotheses have been advanced

* Rasa Gustaitis reported that Dr. Julian Silverman, a psychologist who had worked at the National Institute of Mental Health, was setting up a blow-out center at Esalen.[8]

to explain the cause of schizophrenia, but none has been proven. Some of the ablest researchers and clinicians have sought a cure for this illness. Some patients benefit from psychotherapy, but for most schizophrenics the best treatment now available is to relieve the stress on them by chemical means and by fashioning for them environments they can cope with. To understand how some sensitivity treatment and encounter groups misuse the treatment relationship and the techniques of treatment, I call attention to some of the things which happen in these groups. Typical of the way encounter groups function is this description by Dr. Clark Moustakas, a description which includes his justifications for these procedures:

> The purpose (of encounter groups) seems to be to face openly the forces of dissention, conflict and general evil raging inside many people but rarely given the opportunity for direct expression. The conviction is that straightforward, hostile tactics eventually lead to genuine, authentic transactions between persons, that direct attack and counter-attack, in a climate where the basic intention is honesty of self-expression, will result in compassion and intimacy. The ultimate aim is the development of a positive, loving, human relation. . . . From the depths of anger, rejection and animosity, from the revealing of personal guilt and torture, out of the combined forces of group life, individuals meet honestly and confront one another with conflict and resentment, as well as with tenderness and love.[9]
>
> When individuals express their own convictions, beliefs and feelings without defensiveness or facade, the usual, lengthy time arrangements are not required. Self-awareness, intimate contact with others, and trust, are created suddenly and quickly rather than in a gradual, cautious way. . . . The alienated person is suffering; alone, he is unable to face his estrangement; but in a group, once the alienating thoughts, feelings and mannerisms are out in the open, once they are met, recognized and accepted or challenged, the individual

begins to change; he moves in the direction of authentic presence, dialogue and encounter. The established patterns and habits do not continue, because the alienated self has been honestly shared, and in sharing, an explosion occurs that dissipates the old connections and facilitates new relationships.[10]

When a member of the group is able to express without reserve all of his thoughts and feelings about himself and about the other members of the group, he will be free of his anxiety about himself and his relationships. He will no longer be alone and alienated. The other participants give, without any holding back, all of their reactions to this person. This feedback is proof that he is accepted. It is proof of his acceptance even though the others attack him. This change will come to pass during the brief time of the group experience; no need for the "lengthy time arrangements" of psychotherapy and psychoanalysis. It will be a lasting change; it will overcome the unhappiness and failures of a lifetime; it will give the person a new life—a new ability to love and to be loved.

How this change comes about, if it does come about, is not clear. Schutz uses explanations with a psychoanalytic flavor, but he shows a lack of understanding of psychoanalytic theory. In one passage, Moustakas calls the change a miracle, " . . . the miracle that happens when people are together—intimately, honestly—when they come to be sensitive and loving human beings."[11] Most of the writers state the change occurs because the person is accepted, and he becomes an authentic person when he has overcome his repressions and taken off his masks, and has permitted himself to experience himself, others, his body, the world, things beyond this world.

There have been novels and movies about sensitivity training and encounter, and one of the novels, **The Lemon Eaters,** is the story of twelve persons on a marathon weekend.[12] The description of the novel given on the dust jacket tells us: "As layer after layer of superficial restraint is swept away, each person discovers a self that he or she did not know existed. In the emotional free-for-all that ensues, lives are molded and changed, most of them for the better." The novel reads like a soap opera, but it is a true message to those who believe. Many of those who write about these changes which are supposed to occur see no need for logical and scientific explanations. Techniques do not matter, they say, and the psychotherapeutic techniques taught and practiced by others they consider irrelevant to the person's problems. They do not consider that the techniques advocated by those they consider experts might also be irrelevant, if not harmful.

Carl Rogers is one of the most articulate and scientific-sounding of this group. He writes that there are common factors in most of the groups which bring about change:

> . . . In an intensive group, with much freedom and little structure, the individual will gradually feel safe enough to drop some of his defenses and facades; he will relate more directly on a feeling basis (come into a basic encounter) with other members of the group; he will come to understand himself and his relationship to others more accurately; he will change in his personal attitudes and behavior; and he will subsequently relate more effectively to others in his everyday life situation.[13]

The lack of structure will bring about change. Rogers writes that when there is a minimal amount of structure in the group, the members will move "from confusions, fractionation and discontinuity to a climate of greater trust and coherence." He also writes:

> . . . an inevitable part of the group process seems to be that when feelings are expressed and can be accepted in a relationship, a great deal of closeness and positive feelings result. Thus as the sessions proceed, there is an increasing feeling of warmth and group spirit and trust built, not out of

positive attitudes only, but out of a realness which includes both positive and negative feeling.[14]

If a group has no agenda, if there is no structure, there is no assurance that this closeness and trust and harmony will spontaneously occur. It is more likely that the group will immediately regress and become a collection of hostile persons. The hostility will turn on whichever member of the group offers himself. Many descriptions of encounter show this regression and hostility.

Many kinds of treatment have been proposed and tried for persons with emotional problems, and it would not serve the purposes of this book to go into detail about them. R.A. Harper, in 1959, described thirty-six systems of psychoanalysis and psychotherapy, and I am certain that in the intervening years more systems have been proposed.[15] For our purposes, it will be sufficient to group the various treatments under two headings: (1) those which aim only at the removal of symptoms, and (2) those which attempt to bring about a lasting change in psychic structure. The first group is often called "active" treatment because the therapist recommends actions to the patient, or he performs procedures on the patient, or he modifies the patient's environment. The second group operates through the patient talking to the therapist about himself and coming to an understanding of his illness. This, too, will result in the removal of symptoms. The sensitivity training and encounter groups claim to bring about a lasting change in psychic structure, or, if they believe that there is nothing behind the symptom that needs to be changed, they will take away all of the symptoms.

Relief of symptoms comes about through many methods, through many treatments, and those who prescribe these treatments and use these methods are not always psychiatrists or physicians. Clergymen, teachers, counselors and self-appointed leaders and healers of many kinds administer them. There is an important part of a person's conflicts which comes from his environment. The roots of his conflicts are within himself, but he interacts with others, is subject to pressure in these relationships as well as to hardships in living and working conditions. He may live in or have been reared in an extremely stressful environment, one in which even mature, stable persons will have difficulties. This can happen when there is neglect, deprivation, persecution. It happens in broken families, in the many other tragic conditions which touch most persons at some times during their lives, and which are the constant way of living for others. A change of environment may alleviate suffering and improve symptoms, by giving the person an opportunity to gratify normal human desires and aspirations. In some cases, the damage may have become permanent, and changing the environment does not help.

Many persons cannot cope with a normal environment; can survive only in one which makes minimal demands on them. Some of these persons are seriously mentally ill and are in hospitals; others have managed to have those around them accommodate to their great needs for dependence and nurture. An extremely phobic person finds an environment in which he can be safe from the things he fears; a compulsive person's life is built around his needed rituals.

It has long been known that environmental changes can lessen stress. A stay in the hospital, a vacation, a trip, a change of job can help matters. However, this improvement will last only as long as the environment is without stress.

Sensitivity training and encounter groups use this treatment. Their sessions are often held in attractive, "therapeutic" settings; they advocate that the participants free themselves from crippling and restrictive environments. Many hold that emotional difficulties go no deeper than the symptoms, that there is nothing beyond the symptoms. If the person's maladjustments come from a maladjusted society, then the remedy is to change this society, this environment. This is the way of the counter-culture.

Symptomatic treatment also works through a lessening of

guilt. Guilt—conscious and unconscious—is a part of many emotional illnesses. This guilt may come from doing forbidden acts, often from having thought of the forbidden things. When a person's guilt feelings are lessened through confession and he obtains forgiveness, his symptoms may lessen. Religious persons are helped by this as well as persons whose confessions have no religious meaning.

Dr. O.H. Mowrer is a psychologist who has based his treatment on confession, forgiveness and restitution. A person's conflicts, according to Mowrer, result simply from his past actions of which he is aware and which he conceals from others. The concealment causes the pathology. Relief from guilt does not require that one find the unconscious source of his conflict, for there is no unconscious in Mowrer's system. All one has to do is make the wrongdoing public, by confessing it to "significant others" in his life. Mowrer, so far as I know, is not identified with the sensitivity training movement, but the movement uses this method, as did Alcoholics Anonymous, the Moral-Rearmament Movement, the nineteenth century experiments in communal living.

Sensitivity training and encounter prefer to call it openness, honesty, self-revelation, putting aside masks and roles, getting things out in the open. All of this relieves guilt feelings. The guilty person has a low self-esteem, and when he has obtained forgiveness and acceptance, when he feels that others love him, he can love himself and can have a higher regard for himself. Putting things into words is also a helpful part of confession. When a person puts into words his confused thoughts and feelings, he is relieved. He can often cope with something he has made understandable and which can be communicated to others.

Confession and verbalizing lessen inner pressures. From the person or group to whom the confession is made comes support, acceptance and forgiveness. Leaders of sensitivity training and encounter groups stress this acceptance as necessary for the confession (which they prefer to call *revelation*) to occur. The writer of one paper puts it this way: " . . . the more psychological safety members experience, the greater their freedom to reveal, to explore and venture."[16] Rogers tries to make his encounter climate "psychologically safe" for the participant, so that no matter what he says, the individual will be respected, listened to and considered worthwhile. Because the individual receives this assurance that he will be cared for and accepted, he will reveal himself. This treatment works because of the relationship that exists between the person who confesses and the one who listens and accepts. It is a dependent relationship; its object is a caring, loving, protecting, often authoritarian person.

Other methods of symptom removal work through changing bodily states. The relaxation methods of Jacobson and Lowen which have become popular again, the sensory awakening techniques of Gunther, Rolf and Selver, are among these methods. Muscular tension does not cause emotional disorder, but it has been known for a long time that relaxation of tense muscles produces a temporary feeling of well-being. The touching and fondling and groping and wrestling make some people feel better because these people can, at least for a time, indulge without guilt in pleasures that have been forbidden to them. They can do it because the group or some other authority has given them permission to do this. In the name of overcoming of inhibitions and hang-ups about the body, getting rid of puritanism about sex, they can justify almost anything, even such a gross caricature of treatment as Bindrim's "crotch-eyeballing."[17]

Drugs alter bodily response to internal and external stresses and remove symptoms. They sedate, tranquilize, elevate depressed moods, provide dream-like states and escapes from threatening and oppressive realities, alter perceptions to produce mental states which some like to call ecstasy.

Suggestion is an important ingredient of all of these treatments. The word suggestion used in this context means the controlling of another person's thoughts and actions. Hypnosis is the clearest example of suggestion, and the hypnotized subject's feelings, thoughts and acts are controlled by the hypnotist. Freud learned hypnosis when he studied with Charcot and Bernheim, the most famous neurologists of his time, and he used it when he began the treatments that later came to be known as psychoanalysis. He abandoned it because of its dangers and limitations. Political thought control and brainwashing are other examples of the use of suggestion. The placebo effect of drugs is a well-known example of suggestion. A drug which has no direct effect on the symptom, or even is completely inert, can take away a symptom because the person expects this to happen. People in groups lose their symptoms because they gain the approval of the therapist or the group. They live up to the expectations of the group. They are bullied by persons like Perls and Bach, and gently persuaded by persons like Rogers. One responds to suggestion because he has a need to have a dependent relationship with another and because he has some manner of belief in magic.

These treatments have some value, but the removal of symptoms usually does not last. The original symptoms return or are replaced by others. The new environment may lose its novelty; it may become as intolerable as the old one. Relationships change, and the leader or therapist on whom the person depended and for whom he had given up his symptoms, may no longer seem so magnificent, so powerful, so loving. The dependent person finds that it is difficult to limit his dependence, and his demands for help and acceptance and closeness become impossible to satisfy. Many commentators on sensitivity have noted this dependency, but the sensitivity training and encounter writers do not admit its existence.

Because symptoms return and because dependency is a feature of those methods I have described, and others which aim at symptom removal, therapists have tried to achieve more lasting results. They have tried to change a person's psychic makeup so that he could be free from anxiety and symptoms, and permanently free, without the drawbacks of the other methods. To accomplish this, the therapist needs to help the patient end the conflicts which have caused his symptoms.

The conflicts I refer to are intrapsychic conflicts, that is, not initially or fundamentally conflicts between the individual and his environment, but between forces within him. That is, one set of forces tries to reach ends and obtain satisfactions which another set of forces opposes. Sometimes realistically, sometimes quite unrealistically and unreasonably, the person feels that these forces and urges are dangerous, wrong and should be controlled.

There are many things throughout a person's life which cause his conflicts and which enter into the formation of his symptoms. Of these, the most important are the earliest, for the conflicts all have their roots in childhood. The conflicts concern mastery of instincts and of reality, and they are necessary for development. If the anxiety is not excessive, if the child has normal mental ability, he can cope with these conflicts and can become well-adjusted. Some children, due to excessive stimulation or to events too traumatic for them to handle, or who have been deprived of the nurture they need, will continue to experience these infantile conflicts. They can usually succeed in avoiding crippling anxiety by repressing the dangerous impulses. These impulses they keep repressed, keep from consciousness by means of the neurotic symptoms and character traits. These traits and symptoms are called defenses; that is, they defend the person's psyche from anxiety.

So long as the defenses work well and there is no undue stress from the environment, the conflicts cause no trouble. When the defenses are not sufficient or when a person fails in some life goals or in other ways experiences hurt from his environment, the anxiety increases. Symptoms may return or increase, and warding off anxiety becomes very difficult. Adolescence is one of the times when impulses become stronger, and defenses which worked well in earlier years are likely to be insufficient at this time.

Treatment methods which attempt to do more than remove

symptoms are those of psychoanalysis and the psychotherapies modelled on psychoanalysis. The goal of these treatments is to repair failures in development. Their aim is to make the conflicts conscious so that the person will have a chance to work through the pathological life situations which have caused the difficulties.

These treatments require a long time and skilled therapists. Many persons, probably the largest number of those who need help, cannot obtain these treatments, or they are not suited to their illness. Some persons will not respond to this treatment; they either have personality structures which cannot tolerate the stress of these treatments or their defenses are too rigid and cannot be changed. Competent therapists know that these treatments are stressful and take this into account when prescribing treatment. This is in contrast to the practice of many leaders of sensitivity training and encounter groups who refuse to recognize the limitations of their methods. For some persons, the environment is too diseased for individual or group psychotherapy to be of any value so long as the person remains in this environment. For the majority of people, these treatments are too expensive and too time-consuming. Even if these practical difficulties did not exist, there are not enough trained psychotherapists or psychoanalysts to provide adequate treatment for all who need it and can benefit by it.

Sensitivity training and encounter groups promise so readily what is so difficult to accomplish. They make light of the difficulties I have listed and say that traditional therapists are not successful with everyone they treat because their treatment philosophies and methods are outmoded. Dr. Abraham Maslow, who was president of the American Psychological Association, said that sensitivity training and encounter would replace face-to-face therapy. Advocates of the encountering model see it as essential to psychotherapy. This model "emphasizes health and growth, feeling and awareness of the healthy self, spontaneity and natural response, responsibility for the relationship. The medical model emphasized pathology, knowledge—particularly of the diseased other—and techniques." Maslow told Jane Howard, the author of **Please Touch,** that we need shortcuts and we have to train everybody to be therapists. After he told her this, he excused himself for his appointment with his "regular Freudian analyst."[18]

In all forms of treatment, there is a relationship between the one who treats and the one who is the patient. When a person can express his feelings and can relieve his anxiety, the effect is therapeutic. If the person who listens to him accepts him and does not judge him, he feels better because another has paid attention to him and has not rejected him. Without this permissiveness and acceptance, genuine treatment cannot take place. This is the beginning, the foundation for the treatment relationship, but it is not the whole of treatment. Some believe this is the whole of treatment and, when the climate for treatment has been created and the patient feels that his therapist accepts him, nothing more is needed for real and lasting personality change to take place. It is this type of relationship one person described when he said that a "therapeutic relationship is when you walk in feeling lousy and walk out feeling better." It is a superficial relationship; its reassuring effect lasts only a short time; the contact between therapist and patient will need to be repeated often for this effect to continue. The patient will feel the need to continue to accept the therapist's views, follow his advice and directions. Sensitivity training and encounter groups rely on this type of relationship.

The patient brings to his treatment his past relationships; he reenacts, at least in fantasy, these relationships with his therapist. This action of the patient, in attributing to his therapist the characteristics of persons who have been important in his life and reacting to the therapist as he has reacted to these persons, is called *transference.* It is the cornerstone of the treatment relationship. It occurs in every relationship, not only in treatment relationships. The transference has the most therapeutic value when the patient has no interactions with his therapist outside of treatment, when he knows little about the therapist's personal life and when the interactions in treatment exclude actions and words of the therapist which would create a *real* relationship as distinct from a *treatment* relationship. The therapist does not give the patient the neurotic gratifications he wishes; rather, he helps the patient to learn the reasons for his feelings about the therapist.

These transference wishes and feelings are some of the important matters that are "analyzed" in psychoanalysis and in the psychotherapies modelled on psychoanalysis. In sensitivity training and encounter, nothing is analyzed; self-understanding is sought through experiencing.

In those treatments which are directed towards change of a person's personality, even in good treatment which is limited to symptom removal, the therapist does not have a social relationship with his patient, does not confide in his patients, does not have intimacies with his patient. This is the distance which is a necessary part of the treatment relationship. This distance is often misunderstood. It does not mean that the therapist is *distant* from his patient in the sense that he is cold, aloof, uninvolved, uninterested in him. He has a strong and genuine interest in him, and he is very much involved in the unique relationship that is called a treatment relationship.

Some psychotherapists, as well as practitioners of sensitivity training and encounter, see transference as an unnecessary artificial contrivance of the therapist. The therapist must interact with his patient, reveal himself to his patient—all of his feelings about the patient, his personal philosophy of life, his own feelings, dreams, likes and dislikes. Unless the therapist becomes so involved he is not acting as a human being, the patient cannot see him as human; he is merely playing the role of therapist. Psychotherapy, in their view, is only an intellectual exercise; when the therapist remains uninvolved, it cannot be a true encounter.

One writer, a psychiatrist who leads encounters, says they are "passionate" experiences.[19] Another, also a psychiatrist, believes the therapist and the encounter leader must not hide emotions but reveal them to the group. "Sweating palms and armpits, trembling, irregular breathing, restlessness, flushing of the face—all these and other symptoms of emotional stress in the therapist assure the participants that feelings are really mutual."[20]

If it takes experiencing and encountering for persons to change, if having real relationships is the essential part of therapy, then the therapist will be effective only if he reveals himself and enters into an intimate relationship with his patient. This experiencing approach has been tried by therapists long before the times of encounter, and it has been found ineffective. One of the first to advocate it was Dr. Sandor Ferenczi, a psychoanalyst, one of Freud's first colleagues, and the author of many early papers on psychoanalysis. Ferenczi recommended the psychoanalyst be openly sympathetic to his patients' feelings and allow his patients to express their feelings so freely that "on occasion (he) did not stop short of permitting or inciting certain types of patients to strike him."[21] In this country, in the 1930s, the psychoanalyst, Franz Alexander, tried a kind of experiencing which he called the "corrective emotional experience."

Some writers on psychotherapy and on sensitivity training and encounter take a position that a person can be helped only through a relationship. He is not helped when he comes to understand his attempts to get the unrealistic and neurotic tokens he wants in a realtionship. He is cured, they state, because the therapist *does grant* these wishes. The therapist gives him intimacy, closeness, commitment.

Some call this a "cure through love," and this cure through love can mean many things. It is allied to the transference cure in which the patient gives up his symptoms in an attempt to please his therapist, to gain his therapist's love. One psychiatrist, Dr. Iago Galdston, describes patients who have been severely deprived in childhood of love and care. They have, in his words, a "deprivation neurosis" and they can be helped by a "restitution therapy." This treatment supplies the needed nurture. Galdston writes of the warm and empathic

relationship the therapist must cultivate towards his patients.[22]
A psychologist, Dr. Arthur Burton, believes people grow up
with "missing parts" in their personalities and these missing
parts are the important experiences necessary to their emotional
growth. Through encounter, these missed experiences, or what
he calls the "missed sub-self," can be experienced.[23] Another
writes that in his encounter groups person have a second chance
at experiencing the personal learning they have missed in their
childhood.[24] Dr. Eric Berne, a psychiatrist, author of the
popular **Games People Play,** writes of his system, "transactional analysis," which gives the person the experience of infantile stages of growth and supplies the lost love-nurture of
childhood.[25]
Another writes:

> Perhaps one of my chief traits as a leader is my readiness to
> participate in exercises along with the members and reveal
> my personal responses. For many members who have little or
> no experience with frank and honest sharing of feelings with
> their own childhood families, I offer myself as a person with
> whom they can practice unaccustomed equalitarian, frank,
> direct ways of relating.[26]

The limitations of experiencing are these: the demands of the
patient are unrealistic and cannot be met. The patient cannot
relive his early life, although he can understand its effect on
him. Even this understanding, valuable as it is, never completely removes the damage which deprivation and neglect have
caused. Experiencing love and nurture through the relationship
to the therapists or the encounter group does not last; it cannot
be carried over to everyday living. There is no lasting
commitment to this experiencing on the part of the therapist or
the group leader.
These methods usually do not have a lasting effect because
gratification of the needs does not extinguish them. Many of
these persons have, at least for a time, managed to find people

in their past lives who have given them some of the love and nurture they seek. It has not sufficed because their hunger for this nourishment is insatiable, and those who try to fill their emptiness soon feel drained and weary. The therapist, the group leader, the members of the group, will have no more success in permanently gratifying these persons. The relationship is effective only in some special circumstances. I know some extraordinary persons who have devoted their considerable talents and energy to sustain, not to cure, but to sustain, patients who are too sick to meet the ordinary demands of living. These therapists have an unusual capacity to deal with the difficulties of these treatment relationships. There are also persons who, because of their affection and strong sense of responsibility, give lifelong support to a very sick member of their family.

This does not happen in most therapeutic relationships; it does not occur in the brief life of the encounter group. Evidence of this are the many persons who Miss Howard calls "lab hounds" and who Kavanaugh describes in his article—persons who go from group to group, hopefully seeking this elusive love and acceptance, momentarily elated at the promises of each new group or new leader, looking for better ways to experience and encounter. If sensitivity training and encounter groups could live up to their extravagant promises, we would not have these restless, unhappy wanderers.

Others are unable to love because of the hostile feelings they are burdened with and which interfere with their ability to love. It does not follow, however, that the release of these hostile feelings is enough to make a person capable of loving. In each person there is the mixture of love and hate, the ambivalence of feelings rooted in unconscious conflicts. The release of feelings, which is the goal of many encounter groups, does not affect these conflicts; the unwanted feelings soon return. Because the repression of feelings is often unhealthy, it does not follow that direct expression of these feelings is always therapeutic. It is an oversimplification to say that repression is sick and direct expression of feelings is healthy.

Total permissiveness regarding aggression is no more a solution to conflicts about aggression than total permissiveness in sexual expression is the answer to sexual conflicts. The manner of expressing, as well as the manner of repressing impulses and feelings, has a great deal to do with determining what is healthy. A person's growth is measured by his ability to control the expression of his feelings in a fashion suited to his age and environment.

The release of hostility does make some participants in sensitivity training and encounter groups feel better. They have overcome barriers within themselves and the group has given them permission to say the forbidden things. Not only has it given them permission, but it has told the group members they are doing something healthy and something for which they deserve praise. The notion that the "joy" which comes after the release of pent-up feelings constitutes therapeutic change is a sentimental, romantic and superficial concept of change. It is sentimental and romantic because it enthrones sentiment and ignores reality. "Let your feelings be your guide." "Do what your body says. If you do not, you cannot realize your potential for joy, for openness, for creativity." It is true that creativity and openness involve letting go, involve elements of the irrational and the unconscious, but the use of these elements has to be disciplined.

A serious defect and danger of the encountering method is that it directly attacks defenses which a person needs against anxiety. Schutz derives some of his ideas from Lowen, a follower of the early psychoanalyst, Wilhelm Reich. When Reich published his **Character Analysis** in 1928, he made a notable contribution to the psychopathology of character traits. Some character traits operate as defenses, so that they, like neurotic symptoms, deal with anxiety which comes from unconscious sources. A person who has neurotic symptoms knows often that they are not normal. Yet he needs them in order to contain his anxiety. A person who handles his anxiety and guilt by formation of a character trait does not experience this trait as something alien to his personality, or as irrational, but he finds it useful. Examples are the traits of orderliness and thrift, which even in excess can be put to practical use.

However, the inflexible nature of character traits makes a person less free, less responsive, less creative. He may have difficulty getting close to people and may keep feelings out of his awareness. And he may lack spontaneity. Reich called this state the armoring of character, and those in the sensitivity movement correctly point to this armor and to the masks people assume as factors which prevent them from being open and responsive.

Since the character trait has served the person so well in controlling his anxiety, and has often been very useful to him in his livelihood, he will see no reason for giving it up. He does not suffer, and he does not see the personality distortions and limitations which may be quite apparent to his friends. He does not seek treatment unless the character defenses break down under stress. When he has treatment, change comes about slowly. The psychoanalyst knows a good deal about treatment of persons with this type of difficulty, for today he sees many more persons with character disorders than the persons with acute neurotic disturbances who were seen so frequently in the early days of psychoanalysis. It is possible that many who come to the sensitivity training and encounter groups do so because their character problems prevent them from becoming as involved with others as they feel they should.

Reich's analysis of character was sound, but his technique of treatment was not. He advocated an assault on the character structure. His approach was considered unsound many years ago, yet we find it reappearing in behavior therapy and in sensitivity training and encounter. People can be persuaded and intimidated and conditioned into giving up symptoms and even character traits, but they gain no understanding of the conflicts which led to the symptoms and traits. When the source of persuasion or intimidation is removed, when the effect of the conditioning weakens, the symptom or trait may return, or the conflict may show itself in a new symptom or trait. Or a person with a character disorder may reject these approaches, even strengthen his defenses, when he fears he might lose them. If his defenses are taken away and there is nothing to replace them, he will become acutely disturbed.

The expectation of being loved by the therapist will result in some persons giving up their symptoms, for if the patient is good, and no longer behaves in a neurotic way, he hopes to gain love and acceptance and protection from his powerful therapist. He may also give up his symptoms because he fears being attacked, humiliated, laughed at. Dr. Otto Fenichel writes:

> Medicine in general, and psychotherapy in particular, has long been the role of priests. And frequently it still is today. The healing power of Lourdes or a Catholic confession is still of a much higher order than that of the average psychotherapist. Neurotics, who are persons who have failed in actively mastering their surroundings, always are more or less looking out for passive-dependent protection. The more a psychotherapist succeeds in giving the impression of having magical powers, of still being the representative of God as the priest-doctors were, the more he meets the longing of his patients for magical help. Christian Science and other institutions or sects, which promise health and magical protection as a reward for faith and obedience, may, due to their history and surrounding awe, achieve better and quicker cures than many scientists.[27]

Many psychotherapists have no system of treatment and depend on their intuition to guide them. They do not seek understanding of the patient's difficulties, but are guided by the immediate response of the patient. If their intuition is sound, if they are reasonably well-adjusted persons, they can have some success. If they are disturbed, aggressive, sadistic persons, they can do harm. Many leaders of sensitivity training and encounter groups rely only on their intuition and let their feelings be their guide to treatment. In the following chapter we are able to see the results of their treatment.

The Results—
6 | Good and Bad

Thus far I have written about the sensitivity phenomenon with regard to its theories, its methods and some of its leaders. The methods are not new—others have tried them and found them limited. The theories do not constitute a valid explanation of the way people develop in their emotional life, how they become ill and maladjusted, how they are cured. Many of the leaders are lacking in training and in the qualities needed to help people.

A complete account of sensitivity training and encounter groups includes an assessment of the results. This assessment is of limited value at this time because the necessary data have not been gathered. Many thousands of group experiences have occurred, many hundreds of thousands have participated in them, but there are few reliable follow-ups. The majority of leaders of the encounter movement make no assessment of their procedures for they are convinced their theories are valid, their methods are appropriate and the group experiences are successful. Some biased opponents of sensitivity training and encounter are convinced that everything about the movement is useless and harmful, so they feel follow-up is not necessary. There are, however, some studies and views regarding the outcome of these methods, which are important to discuss.

Dr. Carl Rogers, one of the most zealous advocates of encounter groups, lists several disadvantages and risks.[1] Among them are: the behavior changes are not lasting; people may uncover problems which they cannot work through in the encounter setting; changes can occur in one partner of a married couple and attachments which this person makes to others in the encounter group may be a threat to his marriage. Some persons who have attended several encounters have become "old pros," that is, they have learned the language and rules and they develop a caricature of the hoped-for spontaneity and honesty. This they impose on others in their groups. Other writers have noted persons becoming addicted to groups, making certain leaders all-powerful and wise persons, looking for the latest ways to turn on. Jane Howard wrote of these zealots as "lab hounds," "group freaks" or "sensitivity heads," who

> don't seem to have much of a social life outside the groups. They live, as it is possible to do especially in California, from one group-generated spell of euphoria to the next, savoring the "instant intimacy" some groups are famous for providing. For these people it is old hat to leave matters of friendship and affection and love to chance and chemistry. Not for them the anxious waits for unseen gears to shift from Interest to Like to Love; for them there are shortcuts. A shoulder to weep on, a face to kiss and a body to embrace need be no further away than the next scheduled encounter.[2]

Bertram R. Forer, in his paper, "Therapeutic Relationships in Groups," questions the lasting effect of these apparently intense experiences. His statement is that follow-up reports indicate many have experienced no structural change and remember the encountering experience only as a thrill. Their concept of themselves and their human relationships remain as they were before the encounter. The intensity of the emotional experience is no measure of the real internal change.[3]

Rogers mentions:

> . . . with two individuals . . . the experience contributed, I believe, to a psychotic break. A few helpful individuals have found the experience more unhelpful than helpful. So I have come to have a profound respect for the constructive potency of such group experiences and also a real concern over the fact that sometimes and in some ways this experience may do damage to individuals.[4]

He has reported on follow-up surveys he made of the persons involved in the groups he has organized. He sent a questionnaire to these persons, and 481, or 82%, responded. Of this number, 57% felt that the encounter had made a continuing positive difference in their behavior.

There have been studies, such as that by Matthew B. Miles, on the effectiveness with which T-group training can be transferred to work situations.[5] Allen R. Solen examined the assumptions that learning procedures develop in persons a sensitivity to others and that self-understanding must precede understanding of others.[6] He found that his experimental evidence supported neither of these assumptions, and he concluded that the changes demonstrated only a conformity resulting from group pressures and did not constitute a new emotional freedom. John E. Drotning pointed out that sensitivity training had many similarities to psychotherapy and it may bring out serious emotional problems. He emphasized the need for screening the participants. For groups in industry, he felt the groups stressing decision-making were more effective than those emphasizing personal growth.[7]

Campbell and Dunnette, in their review of sensitivity training, concluded there is little evidence to support the claim that T-groups alter work behavior.[8] Max Birnbaum felt that sensitivity training can effectively influence organizational change, that it is needed to bring feeling into education, but the kinds of groups which stress emotional confrontation and personal growth do not necessarily lead to organizational change. Like others, he noted the risks with inadequately trained leaders.[9] Some authors note that many participants gained an increased understanding of themselves and others from this experience, but persons who have taken part in groups led by poorly-trained or irresponsible leaders have emerged from these groups with damaged self-esteem, with the feeling they have been exposed to the criticism and the attack of others without favorable results.

These and similar studies provide little data and make somewhat broad generalizations on the basis of their data. Of more importance is the work of Drs. Yalom and Lieberman.[10] To my knowledge, this work is the only thorough and sophisticated study which has been done on encounter groups, and it is worth a lengthy summary here. The authors studied 209 university students who were involved in 18 encounter groups of various types, each of which lasted for 30 hours. A control group of persons who were not in encounter groups was also studied. From the initial group, 39 persons dropped out before completion. Of the 170 who remained, 16, or 9.4%, were judged to be casualties. This is a high percentage. The authors consider this to be a conservative estimate of the casualty rate because 25 casualty suspects could not be reached for follow-up. Their criteria excluded a number of persons who did suffer during and after the encounter group experiences, but for whom it could be determined that the encounter group experience did not have a direct relationship to their disturbance.

They judged a participant a casualty if, as a direct result of his having been in the encounter group, he became "more psychologically distressed or employed more maladaptive mechanisms of defense, or both."[11] For example, three participants became psychotic; several had depressive symptoms of varying degrees of severity including suicidal preoccupations; some had anxiety states which ranged from moderate discouragement to severe crippling anxiety attacks. Some persons became withdrawn, suspicious and distrustful of others, avoiding contact with others. Some felt they were more critical of themselves—less accepting of themselves than before the group experience; they felt "empty, self-negating, inadequate, shameful, unacceptable, more discouraged about ever growing or changing."[12]

The persons who were judged casualties experienced symptoms for more than a brief time. An essential criterion for listing a person as a casualty was that the regressive changes had persisted for at least eight months, the length of time between the end of the encounter group experience and the follow-up contacts. If the ill effects lasted for at least this length of time, they were considered to be "enduring."

Of the several findings of this study, the following are the most important: there is a relationship between the type of encounter group, and, specifically, the type of leadership, and the casualty rate. The leaders they describe as "aggressive stimulators" had the highest casualty rates in their groups. These leaders were "intrusive, confrontive, challenging, while at the same time demonstrating high positive caring; they revealed a great deal of themselves. They were the most charismatic type of leaders . . . They asserted firm control and took over for the participants."[13] They were forceful and impatient, and if the participants did not show evidence of change and growth by crying, testimonials, emotional breakdowns and breakthrough of feelings, the leaders pressured them for these manifestations. They wanted immediate results, immediate changes; they did not recognize there is a time-consuming process of "working through" for lasting change and true emotional growth to take place. They paid little attention to individual needs and differences within the groups. They expected everyone in the group to be spontaneous and to shed inhibitions and become free. Although these leaders appeared to be extremely innovative and creative and not bound by orthodox approaches, their lack of discernment of individual needs could only be called narrow, unimaginative, rigid. In the minds of their group, some leaders had a "religious aura."

The groups led by these persons produced 44% of the total casualties, and these were the most severe casualties. The groups which had the fewest casualties had leaders who were supportive. They did not press the group members and rarely challenged them. They were not authoritarian, revealed little of themselves and their groups did not consider them "charismatic." Bell and Howell tapes were used to lead two groups. The setting of these groups was structured, supportive, a setting which did not stress interpersonal conflict. There were no casualties in these groups.

The researchers identified several ways in which the casualties occurred. These were (1) attacks by the leader or by the group, (2) rejection by the leader or the group, (3) failure to achieve goals which were unrealistic, (4) group pressure effects, and (5) input overload. Attack by the leader or the group produced the most severe damage. In the two Synanon-type groups, the attack resulted in the largest drop-out rate of all the groups—10 of 23 members, or 43%. In the situations where attack produced casualties, the leaders freely revealed their own feelings and values and challenged the values and feelings of others. Only those persons who were well-structured adapted to the stresses which caused breakdowns in others. The authors gave the example of one girl in a Synanon group who was not upset by the attacks the group made on her sexual attitudes. She felt the people in her group had come from different cultural backgrounds and had different attitudes toward sex than she did. Because of this defense, their attacks did not make her anxious about her own attitudes.

When the leaders singled out individuals, relentlessly exposing their defenses, the outcome was not always so favorable. One leader harassed a passive woman to get her "in touch with her anger" and told her she was "on the verge of schizophrenia." This woman was a casualty. Group members attacked one man for his passivity and uninvolvement, then criticized him when he began to show anxiety. He, too, suffered a long-term disability.

When participants became casualties because they could not reach the unrealistic goals they set for themselves or which the leaders had promised, it was evident these persons had extreme emotional needs. They had hoped the group would help them to relate, help them break through their inhibitions, help them get in touch with their emotions. Their pathology indicated a need for psychotherapy, and the encounter experiences made their symptoms more severe. They became rigid and inhibited, and in the encounter groups experienced the same difficulties in interpersonal relationships they had in other meetings.

Some leaders recognized the vulnerability of some members of their groups. These leaders were supportive and acted to reduce the members' exposure to group pressures. By their skillful handling of the group, not only did they prevent casualties, but in some cases helped these persons to benefit from the experience. Participants who had high self-esteem did not become casualties. The authors cite "uninvolvement," remaining objective, reminding themselves of the "artificiality" of the group and the distortions of the encounter methods as means some persons used to withstand the potentially damaging effects of some groups leaders.

Extremists and the doctrinaire among the encounter group advocates may say these attitudes are not authentic or show a lack of meaningful relationships; others may judge these attitudes as realistic and sensible. Some group members could

rely on their positive self-concept to evaluate with proper perspective a negative group reaction or a critical feedback. Their center of gravity remained within themselves, unlike several of the casualties who had low stores of self-esteem and whose sense of worth rocketed up and plummeted down with the appraisal of others.[14]

The authors feel screening is essential and they give a list of things to look for in predicting the likelihood that casualties will occur. Persons most likely to become casualties are those who have greater than average growth needs, and who do not have sufficient interpersonal skills to handle themselves in a group situation. The authors conclude their paper with emphasis on education regarding the nature of the group experience, the risks as well as the advantages. The interaction of psychologically vulnerable persons, who seek the "magic salvation through encounter groups" with aggressive, charismatic leaders who make unrealistic promises, will produce casualties.

Five years before Yalom and Lieberman's report, a psychoanalyst, Dr. Louis A. Gottschalk, wrote about his experiences with sensitivity training, and they included being part of a T-group in the Human Relations Laboratory in Bethel, Maine. In the T-group, he saw psychotic and borderline psychotic reactions, depressions, severe emotional breakdowns with acute anxiety, sadistic and exhibitionistic behavior. He wrote:

> . . . the T-group sets up a powerful situation which is capable of evoking many kinds of dramatic reactions in individuals. Most of these reactions involve more than a mild exaggeration of the typical psychopathological traits of the participants.[15]

Redlich and Astrachan, both psychiatrists, have written:

> Such an experience is usually far from neutral. Quite frequently a number of participants become upset in this process; a few individuals whom we observed have become temporarily so upset that we had reason to call their behavior psychotic. Such responses in themselves testify to the powerful processes that occur in groups.[16]

Many persons need to keep a tight control over their feelings and have great fear of losing this control. They are threatened by sensitivity training and encounter. Gottschalk reported that persons who have good ego-strength and high self-esteem "survive the impact of unfolding and exposing their irrational and rational selves and getting stepped on or observing and participating in the harsh limit-setting of others."[17] Those who do not have high self-esteem or good ego-strength are frightened by powerful unconscious feelings and view loss of control as an explosive and destructive event. Further, loss of control diminishes the little self-esteem they possess. The directors of many of these programs seem to take little account of the dangers to emotional health. A number of the participants described by Schutz appeared to be disturbed: Rose who was phobic, Tom who had chronic stomach pains, Nora who had a "feeling of repulsion at her own body." In one place he described some participants as "seriously disturbed people with identity problems, very rigid people."[18]

Psychotherapists are mindful of the suitability of their treatment methods for different patients. Classical psychoanalysis is the recommended treatment for only a limited number of patients, those suffering from neurotic disorders or certain personality disturbances. Although the knowledge of psychological dynamics has been of considerable help to therapists who treat psychotic patients, and some of the techniques of psychotherapy have been used with benefit in their treatment, the evidence is that they and others with severe mental diseases cannot be helped with intensive treatments directed at the uncovering of unconsicous conflicts and the removal of pathological defenses. The condition of these patients is made worse by these attempts. A more directive approach is suited to their illnesses; they often need to be in a less stressful environment: they need to have their defenses strengthened. One of the most successful ways of treating them is with the tranquilizing and anti-depressant drugs.

The drugs alone may result only in tranquilized patients, not necessarily in improved patients. An important treatment means for seriously ill patients has been the "therapeutic community."

In the past twenty years, sociological studies of mental hospitals have shown that lack of attention to the patients' needs for human relationship has contributed to the chronicity of their illnesses. When the nurses and attendants were taught and encouraged to treat each patient as an individual rather than as a chronic, hopeless case, many of these patients who had been judged incurable improved. Many hospitals have become therapeutic communities in which there is truly treatment, not with the emphasis on the interpretation of conflicts and the gaining of insight, but on fashioning a realistic living situation, a living situation which stimulates and encourages the patients and at the same time supports them and does not force them to go beyond their limitations.

There are several important elements in this treatment. One is a permissiveness which has as one manifestation the encouragement of the hospital staff to tolerate a wide range of disturbed and disturbing behavior, and permitting the staff and the other patients to respond to this behavior. The expression of feelings and thought by the patients and staff, together with an informality in their contacts, are important in promoting a community which becomes a powerful agent for change. The staff confronts the patients with their disturbed behavior and its effects on others, but it is important to know that the staff is *trained* to do this in a helpful way. This is in contrast to the assertion of those who believe that training is not necessary.

It may appear that these therapeutic communities are no different from the encounter groups, (and there *are* encounter groups in some hospitals). The permissiveness and the confrontation of the therapeutic community differs in important ways from those methods which are part of gestalt therapy, Synanon games, transactional analysis and similar encounter procedures. It is recognized that the patients are seriously ill persons. They need stimulation and challenges to overcome their regressions, it is true, but the staff recognizes their vulnerability and is cautious about subjecting them to stress. The entire hospital staff is supportive. In the best hospitals, the staff members are thoroughly familiar with the life history of each patient, with his ways of coping with difficulties. They constantly exchange information about the patient, his gains and his relapses, his special needs. In this regard it is interesting to note that, in the opinion of some observers, the Synanon approach is successful not because of the encounter techniques it uses, but because of the emotional support its members receive from group living.

Psychoanalysts, psychotherapists and those who work in the therapeutic communities of modern mental hospitals take great care in the selection of treatment for patients, but in encounter groups the same procedures are used on all who attend, and the groups accept all who apply. Many persons join these groups who should not join. They cannot face the stresses of their daily lives, much less the stresses of the encounter groups. Many are restless and unhappy and lonely, and not seriously ill; others are very depressed, confused and psychotic.

The former president of the National Training Laboratories, Dr. Leland Bradford, has stated that sensitivity groups are contraindicated for people "who are so fragile or neurotic that they spend a lot of their working hours tying to keep in one piece."[19] Dr. Powell, who was a physician-in-residence at Bethel, Maine, said he did not think these groups should accept persons who want to solve their life problems. "If you come here with a life crisis. . . . you're likely to end up with *more* crises. If you're in a crisis at home, then your defenses will crumble under attack.[20] Dr. Martin Lakin, who is coordinator for Sensitivity Training and Group Processes at Duke University, has written: "My own view is that such group experiences are best reserved as learning experiences for normal persons, and best led by carefully trained and qualified persons."[21]

7 | Summary

The sensitivity phenomenon attempts to explain imperfect and suffering man; the sensitivity training and encounter groups promise to perfect him and to take away his sufferings. There is a portion of truth in the ideas of the movement; at times its methods produce beneficial changes.

There are also errors and oversimplifications in its explanations; there are limitations and risks to its methods. It is not that there is another science or movement which has all the answers and the proper remedies; psychoanalysis does not, nor does behavior therapy, nor any other psychological system. The chief fault of sensitivity training and encounter groups is they set goals which cannot be attained and claim results which have not been confirmed and many of which, I believe, cannot be upheld.

Many people do not feel they are living. They are existing, passing the time, waiting to die. They are drifting; feel they have no control over their destiny, feel they have no destiny. They have terrible fears of being alone, even with friends and family they feel lonely all of the time. They want to know: Am I lovable? Am I beautiful? Desirable? Do I matter to others? Some of these people attend the sensitivity training and encounter groups. People who feel they are only half alive will respond to someone who promises to make them fully alive. People who feel alienated, belonging to no one, will grasp at the promise of a new community of open, loving, intimate companions.

Many are concerned about their ability to control their feelings. They have rigid defenses, inflexible modes of living. They find difficulty in being close to others, although they are not withdrawn or antisocial. Often they give the impression of self-confidence and energy. Beneath this exterior they are self-doubters; they feel they are failures. Sensitivity training and encounter writings tell these people they have nothing to fear if they face their feelings of self-distrust.

The lonely people and the apparently confident self-doubters may consider others to be indifferent to them, or are concerned that others do not understand their special problems. They wish to be taken care of. If they have been in psychoanalysis or psychotherapy, they often believe their analyst or therapist is indifferent and non-caring. The sensitivity movement promises them a concerned and passionate leader, offers them a caring, loving, aware community. The leader and the group members interact with them, reveal themselves, frankly tell them what they think of them. They become convinced that all of this means acceptance.

Group belongingness is a necessary part of man's adjustment, and it has always been recognized that the person who is isolated from his fellows is not normal, is either a holy man or an unhappy or sick man. For some, however, belonging to groups, interacting with others, has become the most important part of life. They have mounted an energetic campaign to convince others of this. They have become dogmatic in their assertions and will hear no criticisms of their methods. This is hardly a scientific approach, although they use scientific jargon and the cast-off ideas of science.

Group participation is necessary, but there are many kinds and degrees of this participation. The leaders of the movement do not always heed their own prophets. Maslow, who has given them the concept of the self-actualizing man, wrote that the self-actualizing man is not always interacting. One of his characteristics is that he seeks privacy and detachment. The need for belonging and the need for approval is normal and desirable, but the group can be a force powerful enough to extinguish individuality and personal freedom. The lonely and alienated person, the person who is low in self-regard, the one who is dependent and suggestible, will be led and controlled by the pressures of the group. The encounter group can become his reality, as happens to every addict.

Bonner writes:

> The danger of an indiscriminate luring of persons toward consensus lies partly in its insidiousness. Having yielded to the group's initial pressure, there is a diminishing reason for not yielding still more, until, at last, there remains neither the will nor the logic not to surrender completely. The need for belonging and approval, while normal and desirable in its place, can be so manipulated by group pressures as to obliterate individuality and effective personal freedom. This is the more true when resistance to conformity is regarded as maladjustive and evil. We submit that it is as difficult for the overzealous group dynamicist to become aware of the potential harm to the individual of perpetual group impact as it is for the nonparticipant to realize that his distortion of the motives of others is a product of his isolated existence. Personal and social inadequacy is the consequence of each.[1]

Through the literature of the sensitivity training and encounter movement, there is a strong evangelistic note, a call for everyone to repent of his former ways of living and relating, to take up the new doctrines which will lead to a rebirth in self-awareness, in authentic existence, in honesty and in openness to everyone. No longer will there be facades and falseness; a new morality of sincerity will replace the old morality of hypocrisy and repression.

These are terms which describe religious movements. The

sensitivity training and encounter movement has all the characteristics of a religious doctrine, a belief, a crusade. It exhorts, persuades; it casts out devils and it presses its tracts on all those it reaches. It scolds the unbeliever for his lack of faith and trust, cajoles and forces the timid, derides the doubter. This is the way of the reformer, not of the scientist and therapist.

The aura surrounding the sensitivity movement is not religious in the sense of promoting formal creeds, advocating a moral way of life. It is religious in the sense of those who turn to religion to find the answers to existence and the resolution of all problems, to make up for experiences and relationships they have missed during their lifetimes, to seek a union with the godhead, or a mystical experience. In each age men seek these answers, and in each age they attempt to find the kingdom of God. Is it found in the hereafter, or in the present? Is it within each person, in his vast, untapped potential, and needs only to be brought out? Is it found in those works which have been considered spiritual works—prayer and service, helping the poor and afflicted, bearing without despairing the afflictions and disappointments of life, forgiving, suffering, loving? Or is it found in visions attained by drugs, in ecstasies that come from emotional excitement?

There are many examples of the religious aspects of the movement. Dr. Maslow revealed that after the events of Pearl Harbor he felt his life was changed and he had a mission

> to prove that human beings are capable of something grander than war and prejudice and hatred. . . . All really serious men are Messianic. They have no interest in power or money or in anything but their mission. . . . And a man has a sense of duty to this mission. He neglects his health, risks his life, subordinates all else to his Messianic vision.[2]

The movement is an attempt to create a community for lonely, alienated people. Unlike the early attempts at communal living in this country, it is a community without commitment, and therefore without the possibility of enduring, personal relationships. The result is one more disappointment and rejection in the lifelong series of disappointments and rejections. This is one of the great contradictions of sensitivity training and encounter; it promises real caring and real loving, yet there is no commitment to continuing relationships. One can feel free to seek true intimacy only when he knows it will last. There is also no commitment when there will be no problem of separation and loss. The members of the group can gratify each others' emotional needs of the moment, in the here-and-now, because they have no personal and professional responsibility for each other. This is another contradiction: the promoters of sensitivity training and encounter profess to be honest and try to be open and do away with masks, yet can offer only illusions. What they offer are illusions of loving relationships.

Art Rosenblum, a member of a mystical commune in Pennsylvania, has described the desires of his group in terms applicable to the aspirations of many who participate in the sensitivity training and encounter groups.

We want tremendous freedom; we want to be so free that we could just flap our arms and fly through the air . . . We want to be able to explore all the worlds and have tremendous adventures. We want those adventures to be meaningful also—not just excitement for its own sake. We want to be fully understood—fully comprehended by others, and to comprehend them fully and not only people but all the rest of creation. We want to be free to be fully open and honest about everything with everyone. We want to be completely free of guilt and shame so that we could even be naked in the presence of others and find it natural . . . . Though we long for adventure, we also long for security; the absolute security of immortality, and of never having to grow old and feeble. We also long to have children and bring them up in an environment where they will be loved and cared for by all.[3]

The conversion by means of sensitivity training and encounter would bring ultimate truth, harmony with the self and the world, unspeakable pleasure. Prominent in all of this is the aggrandizement of feeling. Feeling is a part of every human situation, and the sensitivity movement affirms the elements of feeling that are intrinsic to humanness. But reason guides the expression of feelings and the part they play in relationships. The movement often has feeling without reason, a heightening of sensitivity at the expense of sensibility, a take-over of impulse, a frenzy of self-expression.

Whatever faculties man may have—of feeling, intuition or imagination, in vision, trance or ecstasy—can be trusted only after they have been interpreted and judged by reason. Otherwise anything goes: the visions of Buddha, Christ, Mohammed, Marx, Whitman, Nietzsche and Hitler are all on the same footing; and whatever goes best is apt to be blind unreason or brute force. No product of social intercourse is more precious than reasonableness, or more essential to attaining and sharing the goals of life; for love itself is a partial sentiment that often goes wrong, leading to division, jealousy and hatred.[4]

Many have been helped by these programs, and I have considered how they have been helped when I presented the types of treatment which alleviate symptoms and support healthy defenses. In prudently conducted groups, these treatments show promise. Sensitivity training and encounter are still too new for us to be certain in what ways they help and to know which of their ideas and methods will be assimilated by treatment programs. More study is needed as to their manner of changing people, how they can reasonably help persons to develop their potentials, how they can be made part of treatment and educational systems.

The words do not always mean what they seem to mean. Closeness and intimacy are promised, but these do not come to pass over a weekend. One description of an encounter group was that it was a gathering of "intimate strangers." This is an apt phrase, for despite all the things revealed, all the bodily contacts, all the displays of feeling which are expected to produce intimacy, the participants usually remain strangers. Transcendental states and peak experiences are used to describe states which consist of sensory excitement, pathological perception, psychotic thinking. The term "charismatic" had been used to describe a person who has a power to do extraordinary things such as working miracles or speaking in tongues. It is now degraded to apply to those who have an ability to persuade others, who have forceful personalities and often pathological character traits—exhibitionistic, manipulative, seductive, coercive. The language of the charismatic person is a drug which at one time stimulates, at another time anesthetizes. The turned-on feeling that it evokes is a glitter of ideas and a tinsel of feelings.

The goal of some who go to sensitivity training and encounter groups is everlasting excitement without boredom and anxiety; it is life built on the moment, the future as the next encounter. The overly-simplified programs of sensitivity training and encounter are often built on the assumptions that if something is good, more is better; and what applies to one, applies to all. The demand that there be more and more experiencing, that the experiencing be more and more intense, is a dead end. It is no more than a rationale for instant gratification. It is much easier to gratify, to do exciting and novel things than to proceed cautiously and reasonably, to wait, to endure frustration and anxiety.

Finally, the extremes of the sensitivity movement are irrelevant. They are irrelevant to the overwhelming problems of the world. The oppressed and the deprived cannot play, cannot do novel and adventurous things, cannot have transcendental experiences.

REFERENCES

References to Chapter 1

1. Howard, Jane: *Please Touch. McGraw Hill Company, N.Y., 1970.*
2. Clark, Donald H.: *"Permission to Grow: Education and the Exploration of Human Potential," IDOC International,* North American Edition, N.Y., 7: 1970, p. 71.
3. "Encounter Groups and Psychiatry," *Task Force Report I,* American Psychiatric Association, Washington, D.C., 1970, Yalom, Irvin D., Chairman, p. 5.
4. Howard, J., *op. cit.,* p. 3.
5. Howard, J., *ibid,* p. 4.
6. Howard, J., *ibid,* p. 106.
7. Mintz, Elizabeth E.: "Marathon Groups: Process and People" in *Exploration: Encounters in Self and Interpersonal Awareness,* Blank, L. Gottsegen, G. B., & Gottsegen, M. G., (eds.), The Macmillan Co., N.Y., 1971, p. 10.
8. Otto, Herbert A.: introduction to *Explorations in Human Potentialities,* Otto, H. A., (ed.) Charles C. Thomas, Springfield, Ill., 1966 p. xv.
9. Clark, D. H., *op. cit.,* p. 73.
10. Bindrim, Paul: *Psychology Today,* June 1969, p. 28.
11. Roth, Russell: "Nude Therapy Groups: 'a countermovement,' " *Modern Medicine,* December 27, 1971, p. 32.
12. Clark, D.H., *op. cit.,* p. 74.

13. "Sensitivity Training." *Congressional Record—House of Representatives*, June 10, 1969, H4666-4679.
14. Burton, Arthur: "Encounter: An Overview," in *Encounter*, Burton, A., (ed.), Jossey-Bass, Inc., San Francisco, 1969, p. 23.
15. Blank, Leonard: "Confrontation Techniques: A Two-Sided Coin," in Blank et. al., *op. cit.*, 500.
16. Greeley, Andrew: in *National Catholic Reporter*, May 1, 1970, p. 11.
17. Burton, Arthur: "Encounter, Existence, and Psychotherapy," in Burton, A. *op. cit.*, p. 24.
18. AMA Council on Mental Health: "Sensitivity Training," JAMA, Vol. 217, September 27, 1971, pp. 1853-1854.
19. "Encounter Groups and Psychiatry," *Task Force Report I*, American Psychiatric Association, Washington, D.C., 1971, Yalom, Irvin D., Chairman.
20. Yalom, Irvin D., & Lieberman, Morton D.: "A Study of Encounter Group Casualties," Arch. Gen. Psychiat., Vol. 25, July 1971, pp. 16-30.
21. Roszak, Theodore: *The Making of a Counter Culture*, Anchor Books, Doubleday & Company, Inc., Garden City, N.Y.' 1969, pp. 196-7.
22. Burton, A.: *op. cit.*, pp. 12-17.
23. Forer, Bertram, R.: "Therapeutic Relationships in Groups," in Burton, A., *op. cit.*, p. 40.
24. Clark, D. H.: *op. cit.*, p. 82.
25. *ibid.*, p. 77.

References to Chapter 2

Material in this chapter, although not footnoted, has been compiled to a great extent from the following sources:
1. Moral Rearmament Movement, Amana and Oneida communities, and other movements:

    Braden, Charles S.: *These Also Believe*, The Macmillan Co., N.Y., 1949.

    Roberts, Ron E.: *The New Communes*, Prentice Hall, Inc., Englewood Cliffs, N.J., 1971.

    Manuel, Frank: *Utopias and Utopian Thought*, Beacon Press, Boston, 1967.

2. Mesmerism:
 Zilboorg, Gergory & Henry, G.W.: *A History of Medical Psychology*, W.W. Norton & Company, Inc. N.Y., 1941.
3. Group Psychotherapy, Group Dynamics, the work of Lewin, the work of Bion.
 Yalom, Irvin D.: *The Theory and Practice of Group Psychotherapy*, Basic Books, Inc., N.Y., 1970.
 Bonner, Hubert: *Group Dynamics: Principles and Applications*, The Ronald Press, N.Y., 1959.
 Lewin, Kurt: *Field Theory in Social Science*, Harper Brothers, N.Y., 1951.
 Rioch, Margaret J.: *Wilfred Bion's Work on Groups*, 1965 (mimeo).
 Bion, W.R.: *Experiences in Groups and Other Papers*, Basic Books, Inc., N.Y., 1961.

References to Chapter 3

1. Mintz, E.: *op. cit.*, p. 23.
2. Steinzor, Bernard: "On n + 1 Person Groups" in Burton, A., *op. cit.*, p. 66.
3. Brinton, Crane: *Ideas and Men.*, p. 369.
4. Fromm, Erich: Introduction to *Socialist Humanism: An International Symposium*, Fromm, E., (ed.), Doubleday & Co. Inc., N.Y., 1965, p. vii.
5. Quoted in *Explorations in Human Potentialities*, Otto, H.A., (ed.) Charles C. Thomas, Springfield, Ill., 1966, p. xiv.
6. *ibid.*, p. 53.
7. Maslow, Abraham H.: *Towards a Psychology of Being*, Van Nostrand, Princeton, N.Y., 1962. Also in Maslow, Abraham H.: "Fusions of Facts and Values," *American Journal of Psychoanalysis*. 23: 117-131, 1963.
8. Maslow, Abraham H., "Self-Actualization and Beyond," in *Challenges in Humanistic Psychology*, James F.T. Bugental, (ed.), McGraw Hill Company, N.Y., 1967, p. 281.

9. *ibid.*, p. 282.
10. *ibid.*, p. 283.
11. Rogers, Carl. R.: *On Becoming a Person,* Riverside Press, Cambridge, Mass, 1961, p. 276.
12. Roszak, T.: *op. cit.,* p. 240.
13. Gustaitis, Rasa: *Turning On,* The Macmillan Company, N.Y., 1969, p. 86.
14. Clark, Walter H.: *Chemical Ecstasy,* Sheed & Ward, N.Y., 1969, p. 84.
15. Burton, Arthur: *op. cit.,* p. 12, footnote.

References to Chapter 4

1. O'Neill, William L.: *Coming Apart: An Informal History of America in the 1960s,* Quadrangle Books, Chicago, 1971, p. 267.
2. Howard, J.: *op. cit.,* pp. 40-42.
3. *ibid.*, p. 36.
4. Broyard, Anatole: "The Encounter With the Self," review of *Here Comes Everybody, N.Y. Times,* May 31, 1971, p. 17.
5. Gustaitis, R.: *op. cit.,* p. 21.
6. *ibid.*, p. 42.
7. Rogers, Carl R. "The Necessary and Sufficient Conditions of Therapeutic Personality Change," *Am. Journal of Psychol.* 1957, pp. 9596.
8. Rogers, Carl R.: "The Process of the Basic Encounter Group," in *Challenges of Humanistic Psychology,* James F.T. Bugental, (ed.), McGraw Hill, Company, N.Y., 1967, p. 271.
9. Johnson, Richard *Existential Man: The Challenge of Psychotherapy,* The Pergamon Press, New York, 1971.
10. Perls, F.S.: *Ego, Hunger and Aggression,* Vintage Books, Random House, N.Y., 1969, (1947), p. 77.
11. Lowen, Alexander: *Pleasure,* Coward-McCann, Inc., N.Y., 1970, pp. 39-40.
12. *ibid.*, p. 66.
13. Braden, William S.: *These Also Believe,* The Macmillan Co., N.Y., 1949, p. 249.
14. Alexander, Frederich M.: *Man's Supreme Heritage,* E.P. Dutton & Co., N.Y., 1918.
15. Jacobson, Edmund: *Progressive Relaxation,* Univ. of Chicago Press, Chicago, 1929.

References to Chapter 5

1. Wechsler, I.R., Messarik, F., and Tannenbaum: "The Self in Process: A Sensitivity Training Emphasis" in Wechsler, I.R., and Schein, E.H., (eds.), *Issues in Training,* National Education Association, 1962, pp. 33-46.
2. Edward Maupin, quoted by Gustaitis, R.: *op. cit.,* p. 81.
3. Howard, J.: *op. cit.,* p. 42.
4. *ibid.,* p. 43.
5. Mintz, E.: *op. cit.,* p. 13.
6. Blank, L.: *op. cit.,* p. 502.
7. "Esalen, Where It's At." *Psychology Today,* Vol. I, no. 7, 1967, p. 39.
8. Gustaitis, R.: *op. cit.,* p. 135.
9. Moustakas, Clark: *Individuality and Encounter,* Howard A. Doyle Publishing Co., Cambridge, Mass., 1938, p. 45.
10. *ibid.,* p. 54.
11. *ibid.,* p. 67.
12. Stol, Jerry: *The Lemon Eaters,* Simon & Schuster, N.Y., 1967.
13. Rogers, C. R.: "The Process of the Basic Encounter Group," in Bugental, *op. cit.,* p. 262.
14. *ibid.,* p. 271.
15. Harper, R. A.: *Psychoanalysis and Psychotherapy: 36 Systems,* Prentice-Hall, Inc., Englewood Cliffs, N.J., 1959.
16. Malamud, David I.: "The Second-Chance Family: A Medium for Self-Directed Growth," in Blank, L., *op. cit.,* p. 39.
17. Roth, R.: *op. cit.,* p. 36.
18. Howard, J.: *op. cit.,* p. 37.
19. Malone, Thomas P.: "Encountering and Groups," in Burton, A., *op. cit.,* p. 130.
20. Warkentin, John, "Intensity in Group Encounter," in Burton A., *op. cit.,* p. 167.
21. Glover, Edward: *The Technique of Psychoanalysis,* International Universities Press, N.Y., 1955, p. 174.
22. Galdston, Iago.: reported in Frontiers of Psychiatry, Vol. I., April 15, 1971, pp. 1 & 2.
23. Burton, A.: *op. cit.,* p. 17.
24. Malamud, D.: in Blank, *op. cit.,* 38.
25. Berne, Eric: *Games People Play,* Grove Press, N.Y., 1964.

26. Malamud, D.: in Blank, *op. cit.*, p. 40.
27. Fenichel, Otto: *The Psychoanalytic Theory of Neurosis*, W.W. Norton, N.Y., 1945, p. 562.

References to Chapter 6

1. Rogers, Carl R.: "The Process of the Basic Encounter," in Bugental, *op. cit.*, pp. 261-272.
2. Howard, J.: *op. cit.*, p. 33.
3. Forer, B. R.: *op. cit.*, p. 34-36.
4. Roger, C. R.: in Bugental, *op. cit.*, p. 273. also in Hall, Mary H.: "A Conversation with the Father of Rogerian Therapy," *Psychology Today*, Vol. 1, Dec. 1967, p. 64.
5. Miles, Matthew B.: "Changes During, and Following Laboratory Training: A Clinical Experimental Study," *Journal of Applied Behavioral Sciences*, Vol. I, no. 3.
6. Solen, Allen R.: "Interpersonal Skills—A Rejection of Empathy Concept and T-Group Methodology," *Training and Development Journal*, 22: 2-9, July 1968.
7. Drotning, John E.: "Sensitivity Training: Some Critical Questions," *Personnel Journal*, 45: 604-6, Nov. 1966.
8. Campbell, J., & Dunnette, M.: "Effectiveness of T-Group Experiences in Management Training," *Psychological Bulletin*, 70:73-92, 1968.
9. Birnbaum, Max: "Sense and Nonsense About Sensitivity Training," *Saturday Review*, Nov. 15, 1969, pp. 82-83 & 96-98.
10. Yalom, Irvin D., & Lieberman, Morton A.: "A Study of Encounter Group Casualties," *Arch. Gen. Psychiat.*, Vol. 25, July 1971, pp. 16-30.
11. *ibid.*, pp. 17-18.
12. *ibid.*, p. 19.
13. *ibid.*, p. 13.
14. *ibid.*, p. 25.
15. Gottschalk, Louis A., "Psychoanalytic Notes on T-Groups at the Human Relations Laboratory, Bethel, Maine," *Comprehensive Psychiatry*, Vol. 7, 1966, p. 475.
16. Redlich, F. C., & Astrachan, B.: "Group Dynamics Training," *Am. Journal Psychiatry*, Vol. 125, May 1969, p. 1056.
17. Gottschalk, L., A.: *op. cit.*, p. 486.

18. Schutz, William C.: *Joy: Expanding Human Awareness,* Grove Press, Inc., N.Y., 1967, p. 129.
19. Quoted by Howard, J.: *op. cit.,* p. 35.
20. Quoted by Howard, J.: *op. cit.,* p. 35.
21. Lakin, Martin: letter to *Psychiatric News,* American Psychiatric Association, Washington, D.C. November 1970.

References to Chapter 7

1. Bonner, Hubert: *Group Dynamics: Principles and Applications,* The Ronald Press Company, N.Y., 1959, p. 516.
2. "A Conversation with A. H. Maslow," *Psychology Today,* Vol 2, July 1968, p. 57.
3. Rosenblum, Art: *Aquarian Age or Civil War,* Aquarian Research Foundation, Philadelphia, p. 10.
4. Muller, Herbert J.: *The Uses of The Past,* Oxford University Press, N.Y., 1957, p. 362.

INDEX